What people are saying about …

THE JESUS LIFE

"Steve Smith cuts through the religious paraphernalia and daily clutter that obstruct our path to lives of purpose and power, and he clearly explains the simplicity of the Jesus life in the kingdom of God. He has deep insights into how we have come to live the way we do, in church and out. With refreshing realism and wide-ranging knowledge, he helps us identify dear illusions that bog us down and introduces us to simple steps and arrangements that enable eternal living. The directions he gives are self-validating. We have only to 'just do it.' *The Jesus Life* would be ideal for real spiritual progress in small groups in church and in community. Serious individual engagement with it will bring assurance that the life praised in our songs and scriptures can be ours."

Dallas Willard, author of *The Divine Conspiracy*

"Steve Smith always knows where the water is, and in *The Jesus Life* he taps a deep well. It's embarrassing how badly most of us have missed what is at the heart of this book: that Jesus' truth is not only in what He said but also in how He lived. Our age has bred, to an alarming degree, the spectacle of connoisseurs of theology who remain mere spectators of transformation. It has produced more God-knowers than God-lovers. This book is a potent remedy."

Mark Buchanan, author of
Spiritual Rhythm and *Your Church Is Too Safe*

"*The Jesus Life* stands to become the trusted primer on following Jesus well. It's a rich meal, well prepared. Give yourself to this book, and you'll feel like you've got a hand to hold, a cheerleader, and a reliable guide on the only path that really matters."

Paula Rinehart, author of
Strong Women, Soft Hearts and *Better Than My Dreams*

"I hear so many Christians despairingly cry out, wanting to know why they are not experiencing the abundant life that Jesus promised. In *The Jesus Life*, Steve Smith crafts a way back to finding this life. If you are hungering for this life, get this book and read it!"

Bob Arnold, executive director of
Metro-Maryland Youth for Christ

"There have been so many books written about the words of Jesus and what they mean for our lives. This book takes a different course; it is about the way Jesus walked—where He went, how He spent His hours, days, and weeks, and what His priorities were in the midst of a demanding and distracted culture. In *The Jesus Life*, Stephen W. Smith calls us away from our manic, overconnected lives in search of the hidden life—one born out of rhythm, community, and simple service. He guides us through basic values and priorities that echo out of the life of Jesus, helping us discover this abundant life that Jesus describes, yet we so seldom actually find."

Charlie Lowell, Jars of Clay, Blood:Water Mission

"I have made it my custom to search for books that escort me onto the path of deeper repentance…. *The Jesus Life* advanced my steps toward deeper repentance. This book urged me to press truth into the cracks and crevices of my life for a much-needed turning from self and to Jesus. I am thankful for Stephen's good work."

Joseph V. Novenson, pastor of Lookout
Mountain Presbyterian Church

"*The Jesus Life* is a link between knowing Jesus and living Jesus. Steve Smith uses the daily experiences common to us all to guide us into the absolute livability of Jesus. This book is thoughtful and engaging—every page introduces us to a life that is rooted in Someone who is the beginning, middle, and ending of all our stories. After reading this book, the Jesus life became more than a book title. It is becoming an accessible way of life that I long for with renewed hope to be the sum and substance of my story."

Sharon A. Hersh, MA, LPC, speaker and
author of *Bravehearts, The Last Addiction,*
and *Begin Again, Believe Again*

"We've tried everything to live life to the fullest only to find out that we lost the way life was meant to be lived. Steve Smith shows us eight practical ways Jesus lived His life that will help us recover the life that we have lost."

Mark D. Linsz, treasurer of Bank of America

"In *The Jesus Life*, Stephen W. Smith provides a profound new contribution to our traditional understanding of discipleship. When we first come to Jesus, either as a new convert or to affirm a faith we've grown up with, we are asked to 'commit our lives to

Jesus Christ as Lord and Savior.' To this faithful proclamation, the doors of heaven open wide to us. Unfortunately, however, many of us understand this commitment primarily in doctrinal or belief dimensions. No one explained that commitment to Jesus as Lord includes the commitment to His way of life. Traditional discipleship programs teach us what to believe, how to study the Bible and pray, and how to live a moral life, but they leave off how to live it out in a way that leads to abundant life. Stephen W. Smith provides biblical and practical ways to live the abundant life in the way that Jesus modeled it. *The Jesus Life* is an essential read for all new believers, and because most of us never learned this other half of discipleship when we became Christians, it is an essential read for the rest of us as well."

R. Thomas Ashbrook, Imago Christi
and author of *Mansions of the Heart*

"As a pastor and friend, Steve is one of a handful of men who have most impacted my life by leading me to the language of the heart. Steve has always known the traditional church often fails to make us followers of the way of Jesus Christ, and he has fought to guide us into authentic Christianity. *The Jesus Life* gives us practical steps to take back lives that have been hijacked by the expectations of others, ourselves, and culture—often without our awareness. Steve calls us to a consciousness of how Jesus lived and challenges us to small changes that guide our hearts into abundant life. I have lit my 'Sabbath candle.'"

Tim Oakley, counselor, executive coach,
and chief financial officer of iContact

"If you are looking for helpful signposts along the Jesus pathway of life, then look no further. This book will invite you back to your heart's true home … where you will be welcomed, embraced, and celebrated by the Way, the Truth, and the Life!"

Dr. Stephen A. Macchia, founder and
president of Leadership Transformations, Inc.
and author of *Crafting a Rule of Life*
and *Becoming a Healthy Church*

"Steve Smith writes from hard-won experience and an authentic relationship with Christ that invites you to more than absorbing information about Jesus—he invites you to real transformation. From rhythm to ritual, from daily cares to doing good, *The Jesus Life* is filled with the kind of stories that Jesus told—earthy, unflinching, and inescapable. So here's the warning: Don't read *The Jesus Life* if you're interested just in learning about Jesus. This book is dangerous; read it, and you just might end up *living like Jesus*."

Tara M. Owens, senior editor of *Conversations Journal*,
spiritual director, blogger, author, speaker and
retreat leader with Anam Cara Ministries

"In *The Jesus Life*, Stephen W. Smith offers us a Scripture-based, grace-saturated operations manual on living this life to the fullest and experiencing a deepening intimacy with God. It will be one of my staple recommendations for retreats and for the folks I meet with for spiritual direction."

Greg C. Farrand, retreat leader and
director of Selah Spiritual Formation

"Steve always has a way of making Jesus more real while avoiding religiosity. In *The Jesus Life*, he doesn't just give you the words of Jesus and then tell you what you ought to be doing. *The Jesus Life* gives the reader permission to wrestle with real-life situations within an encouraging context that also carries some interesting paradox. One paradox in particular is that of us being conformed into God's image while still experiencing the realities of life's struggles, and this is a wonderful book that helps the reader live within that space."

Dan Maclellan, president of Cornerstone
Benefits, founder of Giving of Life, and
trustee of The Maclellan Foundation

"Stephen W. Smith's *The Jesus Life* is a practical book born out of the author's struggles as well as his successes as a follower of Jesus Christ. He begins with a fresh way of seeing the sanctification of time. I have been particularly helped by the way he uses the concept of rhythm to describe a healthy life of work and rest, of action and contemplation. All of this culminates in a very grace-filled recovery of the concept of the Sabbath rest. However, the most powerful chapter is toward the end when he speaks of the way of suffering. Steve speaks as one who like the Savior is 'a man of sorrows and acquainted with grief' (Isa. 53:3). This is a significant counterpoint to the 'health and wealth' message that is often heard in the church today."

The Rt. Rev. Alexander M. Greene, missionary
bishop of the Anglican Mission in the Americas

THE
JESUS
LIFE

Eight Ways to Recover
Authentic Christianity

STEPHEN W. SMITH

David C Cook®
transforming lives together

THE JESUS LIFE
Published by David C Cook
4050 Lee Vance View
Colorado Springs, CO 80918 U.S.A.

David C Cook Distribution Canada
55 Woodslee Avenue, Paris, Ontario, Canada N3L 3E5

David C Cook U.K., Kingsway Communications
Eastbourne, East Sussex BN23 6NT, England

The graphic circle C logo is a registered trademark of David C Cook.

The website addresses recommended throughout this book are offered as a
resource to you. These websites are not intended in any way to be or imply an
endorsement on the part of David C Cook, nor do we vouch for their content.

Unless otherwise noted, all Scripture quotations are taken from THE MESSAGE.
Copyright © by Eugene H. Peterson 1993, 2002. Used by permission of NavPress
Publishing Group. Scripture quotations marked NIV are taken from the Holy Bible,
New International Version®, NIV®. Copyright © 1973, 2011 by Biblica, Inc.™ Used
by permission of Zondervan. All rights reserved worldwide. www.zondervan.com;
NASB are taken from the New American Standard Bible®, Copyright © 1960, 1995
by The Lockman Foundation. Used by permission. (www.Lockman.org); NKJV are
taken from the New King James Version®. Copyright © 1982 by Thomas Nelson,
Inc. Used by permission. All rights reserved; NLT are taken from the Holy Bible, New
Living Translation, copyright © 1996, 2007 by Tyndale House Foundation. Used
by permission of Tyndale House Publishers, Inc., Carol Stream, Illinois 60188. All
rights reserved; and AMP are taken from the Amplified® Bible. Copyright © 1954,
1987 by The Lockman Foundation. Used by permission. (www.Lockman.org.)
The author has added italics to Scripture quotations for emphasis.

LCCN 2012930187
ISBN 978-1-4347-0064-3
eISBN 978-0-7814-0839-4

Published in association with the literary agency of Creative Trust, Inc.,
5141 Virginia Way, Suite 320, Brentwood, TN 37027.

The Team: John Blase, Amy Konyndyk, Jack Campbell, Karen Athen
Cover Design and Photos: Nick Lee

Printed in the United States of America
First Edition 2012

1 2 3 4 5 6 7 8 9 10

013012

For Gwen, my children, and my grandchildren

CONTENTS

ACKNOWLEDGMENTS

The Africans have a proverb that says, "It takes a village to raise a child." In other words, many people are needed to care for the well-being and formation of an individual child. In Colorado, we have the beautiful aspens that never, ever grow alone. Aspens always grow together and are, in fact, one single tree—all connected at the roots. Since I live in Colorado and not Africa, I want to acknowledge the aspen-like effect of *The Jesus Life*. It takes many people to publish a book, not just the author.

I have the privilege of working with David C Cook, a publishing house that has been successful in the twenty-first century due to the capable leadership of innovative leaders such as Dan Rich and Don Pape. They have championed this book from the initial stirrings to the book you are holding in your hands. John Blase and Jack Campbell engaged with the manuscript, helping me with everything from structure and outline to commas and periods. John Blase offered firm guidance and an expertise that hit the bull's-eye, even though I did not want to hear what he had to say some of the time. The book is stronger because of his work. Both of them had keen insight to improve the manuscript at different levels and perspectives. The marketing team of Mike Salisbury, Mike Ruman, Brian Erickson, and Mike Worley has been instrumental in securing exposure for this book in many areas. Rebekah Ormord, my assistant, helped me research, brainstorm, and find helpful social indicators that I present throughout the book. Thank you to Nick Lee for the beautiful cover that is rich with meaning and implication. And thank you, Kathy

Helmers, my literary agent, for helping me on all levels to convey this important message!

There are other aspen-like people noteworthy of mention, because through their care, attention, and friendship, I have had the unique opportunity to live out the "ways" that I describe in this book: Steve Forney, Chuck Millsaps, John Kapitan, and David Sachsenmaier have all probed at my roots, and together we are living and walking in these ways.

I am so deeply thankful for the supporters who stand behind Potter's Inn ministry. You are the roots of the aspen grove, and without your support, this book and ministry would not be possible.

No voice or soul has been more important than that of my wife, Gwen. She has helped to shape my perspective and explored with me the thoughts before they became the paragraphs and chapters in this book. Together we have lived the Jesus life, and without Gwen, there would not be the richness in the life I am currently living. Thank you for being my soul's companion and helping me become alive to the transforming power of Jesus Christ.

Finally, I thank you, the reader, who I had on my mind and heart in every way I explore in these pages. It is mostly for you that I have written this important book. May this be the primer to help you navigate well the white water of life that will turn your life upside down and inside out to experience the Jesus life.

Part 1

LOSING OUR WAY

RECOVERING YOUR LIFE

We've Lost the Way That Leads to Life

I have come that they may have life, and have it to the full.

—Jesus (John 10:10 NIV)

This book will help you recover your life. The word *recover* means to get back something that is lost. It seems we as followers of Jesus have lost something while on the long journey toward heaven. It's life that we've lost. If you want to really live, then keep reading.

Let me say from the outset that the word *recover* gives us hope. One of the root meanings for this word is from a Latin term meaning "to recuperate."[1] We need to get better. We need to get better at living life—or all we'll do is survive.

We can regain what we have lost. We can mend our disobedient ways and get back on track to experiencing the life God has for us. I would dare say most of us need to recover life in almost every area: relationships, attitudes, finances, past wounds, and life purpose. But there is no greater area that sits waiting for recovery than our life with God. The damage, distance, and disillusionment we experience between ourselves and God—well, it's time to close the gap.

The gap between ourselves and God—the gap between the life we are living and the life we could live—needs to close. Why? Because regardless of what you've come to believe about Jesus, church, and the Christian faith, one thing is for sure: Jesus is all about life. He said plainly, "I have come that they may have life, and have it to the full" (John 10:10 NIV).[2] The full life, the abundant life, life that is "more," a life that is a better, a life beyond what we can dream of—this is what we can recover!

When I was a boy, I prayed a prayer, was baptized, and was told my sins were forgiven. Now that I have become a man, I need Jesus to save me from more than just my sins. It's my *life* that needs to be saved, restored, and recovered. I hope you're nodding your head in agreement. So many Christians today are unhappy, unfulfilled, and disgruntled. The back door of most churches is wider than the front door. People are leaving the church at an alarming rate. We want more than we have been given. We need more than what we're experiencing.

Life is difficult, and through the perils, difficulties, attempts to try this or that, we find ourselves the bull's-eye target of Jesus' own words:

> Are you tired? Worn out? Burned out on religion? Come to me. Get away with me and you'll recover your life. I'll show you how to take a real rest. Walk with me and work with me—watch how I do it. Learn the unforced rhythms of grace. I won't lay anything heavy or ill-fitting on you. Keep company with me and you'll learn to live freely and lightly. (Matt. 11:28–30)

In these pages I want to become your companion in this search to find the way that leads to life—the Jesus life. First, we're going to explore our mortal existence and how we've become so terribly lost. Then, in part 2, we'll explore the myth of trying to live a balanced life—something that is all the rage in books, seminars and symposiums, tweeting, blogging, and preaching. I'll propose a better way by unpacking the concept of rhythm. When we reestablish a life of rhythm, we learn to live to the cadence of the unforced rhythms of grace and a sustainable life. Jesus offers us a life described as "full."

In part 3, we'll look at eight "ways" that breathe life back into us, that sustain us in life's journey, and that nourish meaning, hope, optimism, and a sense of community. These eight ways are all found in the life of Jesus—the very One who claimed to be Life and offers not an ordinary life but an abundant one. These ways are ignored in today's world, yet they are all found in the Scriptures. You'll see that learning these eight ways is not going to be like studying rocket science. They are doable and practical. In fact, they make perfect sense when you see how Jesus implemented them into His life and gave us an example to follow, for it is by following His ways that leads us to the life we most want to live!

I really meant it when I said that this book will help you recover your life. You may want to just sit and reflect on all the things that sentence stirs inside you.

What do you need to recover from?

Has someone or something stolen the life you wanted?

What's not working in your life?

Do you feel like your life and your faith have been hijacked?

What is your part in recovering the life you want? What will God do for you?

✦

Jerry, a thirty-year-old successful insurance salesman, came to me and said, "I feel out of sync. I'm speeding through time zones in my work travels, never feeling caught up, burning the candle at both ends, rushing into meetings breathless, and calling it a 'life.' It's not the life I want." Jerry wants to recover a life different from the one he's living.

Mary, a stay-at-home mom who homeschools three children under eight years old, lamented to me, "I feel like my entire life is on hold. I can't believe that this is my life. My life now—well, it's not at all what I thought I'd be doing back when I was a senior in college and engaged to the man I'm married to." Mary told me that even though the outside of her life looks fine, the inside of her heart is a mess because she resents her children for "disrupting her life." She feels horrible and wants to take back the words she just spoke—but I won't let her have that phrase back. I'm encouraging her to explore this resentment to see if there's a solution, because I believe there is one.

Then there's Paula and Jim. They have a dual-career marriage, both with good incomes. They're influential members of their church and lead a small group every Thursday night. They came and sat down in my office. "There has got to be more to the Christian life than we've been told. We're *trying* to do 'it' all right, but we feel like someone has torn out some of the chapters of the book. We're missing something. Going to church, tithing, and serving feels like it's killing us. We're so bone tired, and we are afraid to tell anyone how empty and desperate we really are. So many are looking to us for the answers." Paula and Jim want more.

Barry came to my ministry's mountain retreat looking for something. He used words like *searching*, *desperate*, and *despairing*. He confessed, "The life I have been living has not yielded the life I want." When I asked him to describe what kind of life he wanted, he used words like *satisfying*, *rewarding*, and *fulfilling*. As we talked, Barry shared the story of man with a good heart who was now shriveled inside like a "sun-dried tomato wrapped in cellophane." Painful to watch and sad to listen to, Barry was about to jettison his faith, stop going to church, and try a whole new and different religion, because "Christianity has not delivered what God promised to me." He went on to say, "The Bible is a book that over-promises and under-delivers. I need something more. Can you help?" I asked Barry if he felt like he needed to recover his life. He said, "Yes, recover. That's exactly what I want to do. I want to recover my life before it's too late."

Our best hope for actually experiencing this abundant life is for us to go back to the One who said, "I am the way and the truth and the life" (John 14:6 NIV). The problem is that many of us have majored on only one-third of this amazing, self-disclosing, God-revealing decree. It seems we have developed a fetish for the truth. Churches offer what they think is the right doctrine instead of helping people discover the life Jesus came to give. We fight over dogma, insisting that believing the right thing will yield the right life. The truth is, the Pharisees in Jesus' day did the same thing so many Christians are doing today. We are on information overload. We go to Bible studies, attend seminars, and listen to countless sermons, but this one reality remains: Information and the amassing of information, no matter how true it is, does not lead to life transformation.

*This is not the age of information.... This
is the time of loaves and fishes.*

—David Whyte

We have believed that the pursuit of truth alone will yield a life worth living, and so we have emphasized doctrine over life, facts over vitality, and information over transformation. Because of our relentless pursuit to get everything right, we've gotten it all wrong.

Transformation is an experience. It's something that happens to a person who alters the trajectory and quality of life from that point forward. It's transformation that we most need to live the life we most want. Paul, the writer of most of the New Testament, was transformed by the experience of meeting Jesus on the dusty road to Damascus. His head was already filled with all sorts of erroneous knowledge. What he lacked was the experience of meeting Jesus. Everything changed for Paul after that encounter. It's my hope that this book will be a Damascus Road encounter for you. I want you to meet Jesus in a whole new way—not just the Jesus who died but the Jesus who really lived! As I've pondered and practiced these ways, the life I most need and the life that is most sacred is returning to my heart. I want this for you, too. As we intentionally practice these ways, we find ourselves not only recovering but also experiencing and living the life Jesus offers us. Remember, Jesus did not come to just teach us new truths so that we can believe; He came to show us how to live.

FIND OUR WAY BACK

I think it is profound that the first followers of Jesus were not called Christians, as they are today. They were called "followers of the Way."

First-century historian Luke wrote about this no fewer than six times (Acts 9:2; 19:9, 23; 22:4; 24:14, 22).[3] Luke described these men and women as "Christians" only one time, in Acts 11:26. I'm not advocating that we change our collective name, but I do wonder if we've lost something important in straying from that original expression the early followers of Jesus used to define themselves. To lose your way can mean only one thing: You're lost.

When the apostle Paul was defending his life and the way of Jesus, he said, "I admit to you, that according to *the Way* … I do serve the God of our fathers, believing everything that is in accordance to the Law and that is written in the Prophets" (Acts 24:14 NASB). Paul's confession becomes a challenge for us today. Do we follow the Way or are we following a denomination, a person, a culture, or a program, or even a church?

If we don't reexamine our ways, then we continue to be stuck like a baby being born breech. The child can't get out of the womb to really start living. My sister was born breech. When she was unable to move through the birth canal, the doctor used forceps to gently help her through. Maybe what we need is a little help too.

ONE MAN'S WAY TO SAVE HIS LIFE

Aron Ralston, an avid mountain climber, slid into a large crater in Blue John Canyon in Utah one sunny day in 2003, only to experience the pressing weight of a huge chockstone slide on top of him and pin him in place. He was unable to escape the force holding him down. One of Ralston's arms was held captive by this massive boulder; it was impossible for him to free himself. He stayed trapped in that dark, isolated sliver of a rock canyon for 127 agonizing hours. After exhausting every known way of escaping, Ralston did the unthinkable: He cut off his arm in order to save his life. His pocketknife became the tool that would set him free. He emerged from the jaws of death after five perilous days. His decision was not easy, but it was simple: to live, not die. Aron Ralston had to choose.

While He was on earth, Jesus issued specific challenges to everyday people who were stuck in predicaments, unable to free themselves. Occasionally extreme action is required for such people to live. Some of the ways we'll explore in this book may seem drastic or so countercultural that you might say, "I can't do this. This way is *so* different compared to how I'm living now." But remember, if it's life you want, then you have to choose.

By practicing the ways of Jesus, we will free ourselves from whatever keeps us pinned down, unable to "move and have our being" as Paul described (Acts 17:28 NIV). What is true is this: It may feel like cutting off your arm to consider these ways and to try to implement them in your life now, but in the end, it could be what actually saves your life.

Alice: *Would you tell me, please, which way I ought to walk from here?*
The Cat: *That depends a good deal on where you want to get to.*
Alice: *I don't much care where.*
The Cat: *Then it doesn't much matter which way you walk.*

—Lewis Carroll, *Alice's Adventures in Wonderland*

If you don't care where you're headed in life, then it really doesn't matter which way you follow. But if you want to *live*, it does; in fact, it matters a lot. It all depends upon the way you take. To find our way back to authentic Christianity, we need to go back to the ways that Jesus "did" His life. The Jesus life is not a set of doctrines or a list of rules to be followed. It is an organic, noninstitutional way of life. The Jesus life is a living, breathing reality that is more and better than what we've dreamed.

JESUS WITHOUT ALL THE TRAPPINGS

In the remote area of Copper Canyon in Chihuahua, Mexico, lives a reclusive people group named the Tarahumara. This tribe has the remarkable ability to run long distances over rugged mountainous terrain quickly and without injury. Their racing method defies the billion-dollar industry of Nike, Adidas, and other footwear businesses that have spent years trying to develop an ideal shoe by filling it with gel, air pockets, rubber, or other secret elements. What baffles logic and scientific research even further is that the Tarahumara run barefoot. That's right! They run on their unprotected God-given feet. In the running world, this tribe is now legendary. Christopher McDougall's best-selling book, *Born to Run*, tells the story of these great long-distance runners. Now runners around the world are embracing the novel idea that to run fast and without injury, all they need to do is run without any encumbrance: no gel sole, no designed tread, and no laces, buckles, or clips.

I share this because when I read McDougall's book, I saw a similarity in what has happened to those of us who call ourselves Christians—followers of Jesus—but who have picked up so many extras, rules, regulations, tips, and techniques about how to live the Christian life. What if we could just go back to the barefoot Rabbi Himself and follow Him to see how He lived His life? What if actually following His simple ways could lead to the life we are searching for?

What we need is Jesus. Jesus without the trappings. Jesus, pure and simple.

There is a long list of add-ons to Christianity these days. Is it the American way? It is the Republican way, or is it the Baptist or Willow Creek way? For a while, everyone seemed to think the way was to be "purpose driven," but that faded away and some other way took its place. Every few years, we hear of another add-on or upgrade, but we keep coming up empty.

Our cultural obsessions with excellence, production, and customer satisfaction have invaded the way we do church these days, yet when you rethink these corporate norms, you don't see Jesus concerned with any of it. For Jesus, it was about obedience, not excellence. For Jesus it was never about moving toward greatness or mega-ness. He was focused on the few, the small, the overlooked, and the insignificant. Jesus had a soft spot in His heart for the outsider and stooped to honor children, women, and those marginalized by the culture. Have we allowed culture and business to shape our way? If so, having the courage to reestablish the ways of Jesus would be a good start to living our lives and following Him in the simple and unadorned ways He demonstrated.

Living the Jesus life is not about trying to be more religious and devout. Adherents of the world's major religions—Buddhism, Hinduism, Judaism, and Islam—are all about trying harder to gain a higher power's acceptance. Not so as a follower of Jesus. It's not about trying harder until you "get it." We follow Jesus' ways through simple acts of implementing His practices into our lives.

THE JESUS LIFE IS NOT THE CHURCH LIFE

Church historian Alfred Loisy wrote, "Jesus came preaching the kingdom of heaven. What he got was the church." When we do the math, we realize that is true. Jesus came speaking and teaching about the kingdom of God or the kingdom of heaven; He spoke the term *kingdom* eighty-seven times, recorded by all four gospel writers combined. Yet all four writers have Jesus speaking the word *church* only two times. And in the book of Acts, Luke said plainly, "After his suffering, he presented himself to them and gave many convincing proofs that he was alive. He appeared to them over a period of forty days and spoke about the *kingdom of God*" (Acts 1:3 NIV). Jesus taught us about living in the kingdom. He told us to "seek first the kingdom of God" (Matt. 6:33 NKJV).

But something has gone wrong. When church talk replaces Jesus talk, when church power struggles replace struggles against principalities and powers of this world, when church emphasis usurps devotion to Jesus, we have lost ourselves and left the Jesus way. The church life squeezes Jesus not only out of our vocabulary but perhaps out of our hearts as well.

Drive across the landscape of America on a typical Sunday morning and you will find small, medium, large, mega, and multisite congregations that are gathered together to ask the Lord's blessing. However, 80 percent of churches in America are declining in attendance. We may be leaving disgruntled, but do we even know the direction to head next? Something is missing.

Key findings in a recent nationwide survey revealed that people in America ages eighteen to twenty-nine are giving up on the church:

- Sixty-five percent rarely or never pray with others, and 38 percent almost never pray by themselves either.
- Sixty-five percent rarely or never attend worship services.
- Sixty-seven percent don't read the Bible or sacred texts.

Dr. Thom Rainer, president of LifeWay Christian Resources, said, "We have dumbed down what it means to be part of the church so much that it means almost nothing, even to people who already say they are part of the church."[4]

✦

The life God wants us to live is dependent on the way we live. It's anchored in the way Jesus lived His life. Peter, one of the original followers of the Way, began his life as a fisherman, but as he followed Jesus, everything changed for him. He was transformed from an insecure man into an ardent follower of Jesus. He wrestled with power issues but learned in following Jesus that the life-giving way to lead is to serve. It is Peter who shared these words in his letter to young and eager followers of Jesus: "This is the kind of life you've been invited into, the kind of life Christ lived. He suffered everything that came his way so you would know that it could be done, and also know how to do it, step-by-step" (1 Peter 2:21). Real life has a real way to follow. It's the Jesus way with the Jesus truth that yields the Jesus life.

I'm so relieved that Peter reminded us that this life we want can be experienced! Further, we can "know how to do it, step-by-step!" So, this life is doable, attainable, and not impossible. It's not out of our reach. It is a step-by-step journey of practicing the ways of Jesus so that we can live the life He promised to give us. Each step will require a reexamination of our lives, and we will have to make some difficult choices.

WHAT IF YOU COULD IMPROVE YOUR LIFE BY 25 PERCENT?

When my wife and I sit with couples who come to our retreat because they are tired, worn out, and burned out on religion, we remind them that the life they thirst for is not a life of perfection or of finally attaining a plateau. We speak and coach our visitors to seek a 25 percent improvement in their lives. At first, you might think that's not much at all and perhaps not worth the time and focus. But let me encourage you to think about this way.

Remember when you were in school and the teachers marked your papers and tests scores with a grade—A, B, C, or D, or an F for failing? In school, a 25 percent improvement moved you from a D to a B, or from an F to a C. Apply that kind of change to life and 25 percent moves you from poor to above average, from failing at life to really living your life. Who of us would not be satisfied in our lives with an improvement of 25 percent or perhaps more? By implementing and practicing these ways, I am confident not only that your life can improve but also that the life that needs to be recovered can and will be.

As we go from here, I'm going to share how Jesus lived His life according to each of the eight ways. Then, I will tell some true stories of ordinary men and women I've met who have experienced the transformation they most wanted in their marriages, careers, families, and hearts by practicing these ways. Finally, in each chapter, I will give you practical, step-by-step ideas of how you can implement these Jesus ways into your own life so you can recover what's been lost. I want you to start living. So let's get started.

1. Read Jesus' words in Matthew 11:28–30. Try reading these verses from various translations. Circle or underline the words that stand out to you.

2. This chapter presents three key questions about recovering your life. Take some time to answer these questions perhaps by journaling your thoughts and sharing them in your group or class:

    a. What do you need to recover from?

    b. Has someone or something stolen the life you wanted?

    c. What's not working for you in your life?

Part 2

WALKING IN THE WAY

THE RHYTHM OF JESUS

Living a Life That Sustains

There is a time for everything, and a season
for every activity under the heavens.

—Ecclesiastes 3:1 (NIV)

People today seem to have an unprecedented thirst to know how
to make life work. Best-selling author and leadership guru Stephen
Covey stated, "The challenge of work-life balance is without question one of the most significant struggles faced by modern man."[5]
We are demanding, yearning, and pleading to know how to make
life work better.

Yet in the very lifestyle of Jesus we find the solution. Anchored
in the Bible, steeped in Jewish ways, embraced by Jesus Himself, and
practiced by the New Testament church, the answer to the dilemma
we have been living is found in one word: *rhythm*.

The Jewish prophet Jeremiah lamented over this forgotten
principle:

> Cranes know when it's time to move south for win-
> ter. And robins, warblers, and bluebirds know when
> it's time to come back again. But my people? My
> people know nothing, not the first thing of God
> and his rule. (Jer. 8:7)

Unlike the cranes, robins, warblers, and bluebirds, we have forgotten, ignored, and thumbed our noses at the concept of rhythm. Now we are wired, always on, always available, and always busy.

Recently I visited the branch manager of my bank to ask a question. While I waited in her office, I noticed a framed card on her desk:

> Every morning in Africa, a gazelle wakes up. It knows that it must run faster than the fastest lion or be killed. Every morning a lion wakes up. It knows that it must outrun the slowest gazelle or starve. It doesn't matter whether you are a lion or a gazelle. When the sun comes up, you'd better be running.

The card sat prominently on her desk as a daily reminder of what her employer deemed important: running! Is that all we can do? Run and hunt like crazy every day just trying to survive? The prophet was right; we don't know anything.

We try to convince ourselves we're marching to the beat of our own drums when the truth is we're chasing the wind and reaping the whirlwind. Some of this is connected to our toys, aka modern technology. We're constantly connected—always checking to see who might have emailed, texted, or posted on Facebook. We might be "needed," so we keep ourselves plugged in—wired 24/7. For many of us, always being on leaves us feeling completely off. It's insane. Breathless living is anything but the abundant life. The pace at which we live is not sustainable.

Nick showed up in my office one day and said, "I live my life in fifth gear all the time. I am speeding through life, fulfilling tasks and meeting everyone else's agenda but have no time for myself. Is there any help for me?"

I asked him, "Do you think you have *a third gear* within you?"

He grinned and replied sheepishly, "I think I've stripped my second, third, and fourth gears. Fast is all I know."

In order to recover your life, you first need to recover your rhythm. The writer of Ecclesiastes, said to be the wisest of all men, wrote a beautiful rhythmic poem to describe the cadence of our lives.

> There is a time for everything,
> and a season for every activity under the heavens:
> a time to be born and a time to die,
> a time to plant and a time to uproot,
> a time to kill and a time to heal,
> a time to tear down and a time to build,
> a time to weep and a time to laugh,
> a time to mourn and a time to dance,
> a time to scatter stones and a time to gather them,
> a time to embrace and a time to refrain from
> embracing,
> a time to search and a time to give up,
> a time to keep and a time to throw away,
> a time to tear and a time to mend,
> a time to be silent and a time to speak,
> a time to love and a time to hate,
> a time for war and a time for peace.

> What do workers gain from their toil? I have
> seen the burden God has laid on the human race.
> He has made everything beautiful in its time. He
> has also set eternity in the human heart; yet no one
> can fathom what God has done from beginning to
> end. I know that there is nothing better for people
> than to be happy and to do good while they live.
> (Eccl. 3:1–12 NIV)

God's intent is for His creation to live according to a basic, sustainable rhythm that produces life. This sacred cycle is seen in nature, as seeds germinate, animals mate, and human beings age. We can receive our days as gifts from God and find Him in each one, or we can squander them as if they can easily be replaced. A life of rhythm helps us tell time rather than let it imprison us. Living in healthy rhythm allows us to experience more of the abundant life, mindful of God's faithfulness every day.

JESUS AND RHYTHM

As a boy, Jesus was raised in a culture of sustainable rhythm. His soul was shaped by the cadence of Sabbath keeping and seasonal festivals that were intended to help Him and all people to remember God's faithfulness, protection, and provision. Luke 4:16 tells us that Jesus observed the Sabbath "as was his custom" (NIV). For thirty years, even before He started His ministry, He lived according to a 6:1 rhythm: He worked six days, then rested one. He stopped His work and ceased His routine. He enjoyed His family. And He worshipped His heavenly Father and did not defy the cadence of life that God initiated.

We also learn that Jesus' family was observing one of the seven Jewish festivals[6] when Mary and Joseph discovered that Jesus was missing. For three days they could not find their boy among the bands of pilgrims who were returning home after the festivities in Jerusalem. Luke's gospel reminds us, "*Every year* Jesus' parents traveled to Jerusalem for the Feast of Passover" (Luke 2:41). But this trip had a kink in it. Mary and Joseph went on a search to find their child only to discover Him back in Jerusalem with the teachers of His faith. Jesus was learning, exploring, and being exposed to the depths of His awakening life in God.

Jesus' life is marked with this cadence of a sacred rhythm. There was no sense of the tyranny of the urgent in Jesus' life. His life was shaped and formed by a rhythm that was etched in His culture and His heart. He used the marking of the feasts to share some of His greatest teachings and insights into the spiritual life. Jesus marked His own "Last Supper" when observing one of the feasts again in His life. It was there that Jesus used the Passover meal and changed it by offering new insight with the symbol of the bread and the cup. Jesus even told us to remember His life and death by observing this feast, which followers of Jesus practice in taking Communion or serving the Lord's Supper. This regular rhythm of remembering and worshipping anchors our faith in the life and death as well as the teachings of Jesus Christ. Jesus lived His life according to a rhythm that we seem to have missed while focusing on His teachings and neglecting His lifestyle and the way that He "did" His life.

SOMETHING IS WRONG!

Laurie and Ben came to talk with me about the speed and intensity of their lives. They felt "out of control." As I listened, they explained that their pastor wanted Ben to serve as an elder, a lay leader in their church—something Ben really felt honored to be invited to do. But he was wondering where the extra time was going to come from to do something of that magnitude. Laurie's eyes welled up with tears. She said, "We're basically happy in our marriage and life, but I feel like one more thing is going to push us over the edge, especially Ben, who already works a lot of hours and often comes home late."

As we continued talking, it became apparent that Ben was going to accept his pastor's invitation more out of guilt—"What would he think of me if I turned it down?"—rather than his own desire at this particular time in his life. Laurie and Ben are learning what many of us face. Good opportunities will keep coming to us, but do we have to do everything? Is there a way to choose a few things and do them well rather than do a lot of things halfway or not at all? Can we accept the fact that we may be in a season when we need to say no with the understanding that the season will not last forever?

We have little rhythm in our calendars and sometimes are afraid to take time off from our work, because someone is right behind us ready to fill in our place if we step out. Time is marked by Halloween, Santa Claus, presidents' birthdays, and the Easter Bunny. The year is divided by the last mail pickup on April 15—the day most Americans pay their taxes. Time flows only horizontally from one event to the next. There's no time to observe the vertical events, the transcendent events where God breaks through and alters our lives forever. Events that shape our lives—when we first became Christians, our baptisms, or our anniversaries of major life events—seem forgotten for most. We have little to no sense of transcendence in our schedules.

What if our twenty-first-century "festivals" could include baptism anniversaries, anniversaries of our decision to follow Jesus, times to celebrate milestones in life such as joining a small group, becoming a member of a church, and more? After all, the Bible tells us not only to weep with those who weep but also to rejoice with those who rejoice (Rom. 12:15). Regular times of rejoicing can really help! *The Message* Bible puts it this way: "Laugh with your happy friends when they're happy." With so much pain and sadness in the world, what is wrong with spreading a little bit of joy?

A life out of control, a life spinning on the hamster wheel, and a life running on empty are all indicators that something is wrong. We want "it" all, but the problem is that the "it" keeps changing; the bar we have to jump over to succeed keeps getting higher, and then there's the shame we wallow in when we fail, get rejected, and can't measure up. Something is missing.

Rhythm is missing. Rather than trying harder to do it all better, how can we discover a rhythm in our living that is sustainable and life-giving?

Our problem with the famous verse from Ecclesiastes about there being a "time for everything" is that we want everything crammed into *now*, and we simply do not like to wait for the next "time" to come around.

Have we forgotten who we are as human beings, created in the image of God and the very beloved of God? Do we have to live by a standard that robs us of our souls as image bearers of God and lowers us to teeth-baring, annihilating creatures? This is the lie we've bought, whether in the form of the American dream or the church dream or some other vision. It's all an illusion.

Can you imagine your life with less stress, less fatigue, and less discouragement? How about more peace, more hope, and more joy?

THE LIGHTBULB CHANGED EVERYTHING

Up until the Industrial Revolution beginning around 1830, American and European cultures were based on agriculture and farming. The changing seasons of the year dictated what could be grown and when it would be harvested. People paced their lives on an agricultural rhythm of springtime planting, summer growing, and fall harvest. They rose with the sun and worked until the sun went down because there simply was no light, except candles that gave minimal light in homes and workplaces.

The dawn of the Industrial Revolution and the massive spread of machines changed that natural rhythm. To keep up with an ever-growing demand for labor, children as young as six years old entered the workforce. Harnessing electricity and the all-important lightbulb later in the nineteenth century changed the pulse of living. In 1879, Thomas Alva Edison produced the first commercially available lightbulb in America. By 1890, Edison had wired one square block of New York City, making it the center of a changing world. With the spread of the lightbulb, bedtimes changed. People stayed up later and accomplished more. Factories implemented shift work. The machines rarely ceased, and people lined up to work to gain prosperity and a better way of life.

In the latter part of the twentieth century, another light dawned—the Internet, perhaps changing our lives as much as the lightbulb did a century before. Computers, now weighing only a pound or two, make commerce, information, and communication lightning fast. We live at the speed of nanoseconds, tied to our smart phones and constantly available. We may be moving, but there's no rhythm. And where there's no rhythm, there's little living.

LACK OF RHYTHM HAS DIRE CONSEQUENCES

In my work with leaders in the marketplace and ministry, one thing has become clear: Most problems in relationships, work, and health can be traced back to this lack of rhythm, an absence of a varied tempo in living life. In our abuse of the God-given rhythms, we allow ourselves to fall victim to our culture's pouring us into its own mold. I find it fascinating to ask a business leader or church leader, "How many hours do you think you work a week?" The replies seldom reflect the truth. Most of the time they fudge on the actual number of hours until I ask them to chart out a normal week. Then the "lights go on." When I asked Joe, an insurance salesman, he quickly said, "Fifty hours is my normal week." But when we charted this out, counting the times he checked his email from home and answered his voice mail calls, the fifty suddenly became seventy hours. Joe didn't quite know what to say. Unfortunately, Joe's seventy is nothing compared to others.

The antidote for twenty-first-century living is not necessarily going back to the farm but learning to live in rhythm. It's true that we will never be able to return to the "olden days" or the "golden days." We don't have to. We can, however, return to rhythm, and a life of rhythm will sustain and replenish our lives.

MY EPIPHANY TO SEE ANOTHER WAY

During the darkest time of my life, I went to a monastery to speak with author Dallas Willard. I lived there for a month. If that sounds desperate, that's because it was. I was tired, worn out, and edging on burnout. I was miserable. Nothing was working. Or maybe life as I had known it was not working. As I look back on that experience, I can now clearly say the monastery time was a divinely conspired intervention program God orchestrated to show me a better way to live. I could not have found this way on my own. I needed someone to guide me into the ways of Jesus—the way Jesus did His life. It was in those conversations with Dallas Willard that I morphed from the inside out and was challenged to rethink everything I was doing and believed. It altered the trajectory of my life.[7]

Prior to my time at the monastery, my life was not working; in fact, it wasn't much of a life at all. I violated any possible rhythm by driving my body like an ever-ready ambulance to any crash victim of life that might be in trouble. My marriage was in shambles because of my drivenness and workaholism. I gave 110 percent of myself to my work and offered only a fatigued, worn-out, tattered shell of a man to my wife. I gave the best to my work and the worst to my wife and four young children.

On the first day in that monastery, my mentor simply said, "I am here to tell you that it is actually possible to live like Jesus." I suppose the reason his words are etched in my soul is that I had almost given up believing such a thing was even possible. "Live like Jesus"—I think I had forgotten that living like Jesus was supposed to be the goal in life.

JESUS CAME TO HELP US LIVE

I knew how to live the church life, the American life, and the Baptist life. But I had to face the fact that I did not know how to live the Jesus life. To begin with, I had to personally destroy a common myth.

The myth of a balanced life leads to a downfall in life. This modern American myth says, "We can have it all—we just have to balance it all!" Go to any bookstore or open any magazine and you'll find a plethora of words about finding balance in life. But we've been duped. The real truth is, as one writer put it, "balance is bunk. It is an unattainable pipe dream.... The quest for balance between work and life, as we've come to think of it, isn't just a losing proposition; it's a hurtful, destructive one."[8]

As a child, my father would take me to the circus every year. It was an annual treat to go and watch the elephants, clowns, and stunts. One of the acts I'll never forget was the man who spun dozens of white china plates on small rods. A woman would hand him one plate after another, and his goal was to spin as many plates as possible. Every plate wobbled and bobbed until the man could rush over and move the small dowel rod to keep the plate in the air. I remember squealing for him to rush to the one he wasn't noticing and keep it from shattering on the ground.

It was all about balance. Keep all the plates spinning and you'll gain the crowd's applause. We've taken that circus act and tried to live it out now for decades. We've attended seminars, read books, and digested articles that promise to help us spin all our demands: work, spouse, children, money, in-laws, church, etc., so that no plate crashes. But the broken pieces of our lives all over the ground indicate balance isn't all it's promised to be.

Life is not about balance; it's about rhythm.

One of the central problems with attempting to live a balanced life is that Jesus never commanded or encouraged us to such living. It's not in the Ten Commandments or the eight Beatitudes, and none of the prophets cried out for a more balanced life.

On the other hand, the Bible does give us a picture of a life lived in rhythm, a way of walking in a cadence that breathes the abundant life, not the busy life. The rhythm that offers us life is not a human-made rhythm, no matter how sophisticated and techno-savvy we become. The rhythm that breathes life is a sacred rhythm—one created by God from the very beginning of time.

HOW TO LIVE IN RHYTHM TODAY

As you think through the rhythm for your life, you may find that changing your mind-set is easier than you assumed. It simply requires an honest look at the life you are presently living, admitting truthfully to yourself and to some close friends how you're living right now (work hours included), and asking God for the courage to walk in the new way and to live this out step-by-step.

Start with Sabbath keeping.[9] Experiment with this ancient practice of ceasing work and perhaps even ceasing being so available. Stop using technology for one day a week and see if you can survive. Change your voice mail to say, "Hello. You've reached Steve on his Sabbath day. I'm not available to call you back until tomorrow. Please leave your number and you'll hear from me in twenty-four hours—maybe sooner." Don't check your email on Sundays. I've found that even in the simple notion to just check and see if someone wrote or needs me that I am lured into minutes that become hours. When I had intended to unplug, my mind is now active, my soul is plugged back in, and I'm thinking about work, not about how much I'm enjoying my friends, my Sabbath meal, or my hike on my favorite trail.

Consider what the modern-day equivalent might be for you to begin enjoying some twenty-first-century festivals—times of celebrating, feasting, and enjoying. By having certain times marked and observed, you'll find a rhythm of expecting and anticipating a time away with a life-giving friend or a season of rejuvenation with your spouse.

When I talked to one of my closest friends about our need to get together more regularly, we took out our calendars and marked a date—exactly one year from the time we were together then—when we would be together, enjoy hiking, talking, praying, and sharing the journey together. This special man is one of my most life-giving friends. Why would I not want an annual time together? We live two thousand miles apart and can see each other only once a year. But what if our time could become our "annual pilgrimage of friendship"? It's set now for us to do this—with the blessing of our wives because they know we are better men, better husbands, and better fathers for having this special time. Creative ideas such as family reunions, getaways with spouse, quarterly weekend retreats, or a monthly day of soul care and reflection can all become twenty-first-century ways of living according to a rhythm that sustains and replenishes rather than a lifestyle that drains and leaves us feeling empty.

How could your family plan a quarterly time away from your normal routine and do something fun, exciting, and life-giving? Perhaps let each member of the family plan the weekend or a twenty-four-hour excursion. Tom might want to go to the beach for a campout. Mary might want to do a day of shopping in the city and eat at a new restaurant. The idea here is to talk, explore, and imagine some life-giving events that you can participate in. Try it and see what happens.

One church I know of implemented a Year of Jubilee—a year of freedom described in the Bible where debt was forgiven and life could start over. To do this, the leaders of the church decided to cancel every church service and unnecessary committee meeting for a whole year. They offered only worship services. No Sunday school. No small groups. No meetings. It revolutionized the way the congregation saw themselves. It made them want to focus on the major things of their faith and let the minor things fall off people's calendars.

Consider these ideas to implement life-giving rhythms into your life:

1. Ask a group of life-giving friends to join you once a month for a meal where everyone brings a dish of food and shares or where everyone meets at a restaurant.

2. Plan a Sabbath dinner one evening where friends gather for a time of fellowship and good food. At the beginning of the time together, ask the guests to write on a piece of paper something they want to cease from during the Sabbath celebration. One might write, "Worrying about my debt." "Thinking about my impending layoff from work." Have each guest place his or her paper in a box labeled "Sabbath." Someone might even decide to put a watch, credit card, or car keys in the box as a symbol of something that needs to stop for this particular Sabbath. Light a Sabbath candle and enjoy!

3. If you're in a small group, let the group brainstorm ideas of fun and life-giving festivals.

Calendar these times in advance so people can prepare. One small group I know of decided to go camping one weekend to observe the Jewish Festival of Booths, during which Jews left their homes and lived in tents to remind themselves of the exodus and God's provision and faithfulness. The camping trip can be a time of remembering God's faithfulness and allowing each member to share "How God has been faithful to me this past year."

4. Explore with your church leaders the annual rhythm of life of the church. Can you rethink any aspects? Can you postpone or cancel any events? How can the entire church begin to embrace the rhythm of Sabbath, and what might this look like for a church family to experience together?

5. Plan an annual spiritual retreat. Look for offerings in your area you can attend that will refresh and renew you and some of your family and friends.

6. Find a spiritual director with whom you can have guided conversations about your life, lifestyle, rhythm, relationship with God, and personal desires to live a better life. Try to meet monthly with this person to gain wisdom, insight, and accountability in making progress in your life.

7. Read some books and articles on rhythm, chrono-biology, or time. Some suggestions are found on my ministry's website: www.pottersinn.com.

8. Make a decision to read the gospel of Luke, and begin to mark and journal the lifestyle of Jesus. Do this with some friends or in your small group and share the insights you gain.

9. Create a chart showing the seven days of the week. Insert blocks denoting times you do certain things: work, cook, clean, exercise, small group, and church. Gain an honest understanding of the rhythm of your actual week. Now make another chart, this time showing how you'd like your week to look. List the steps you need to take toward making your life the way you want it to be.

10. Read Ecclesiastes 3. Ponder through each of the time seasons that are mentioned. What time is it for you right now? What season are you going through? Where do you think you're headed in your life? Be specific. Do this in a group and share. Use the language of Ecclesiastes 3 to help you understand the many metaphors in life this chapter has offered.

In an effort to find a life-giving cadence, many followers of Jesus are now returning to the roots of our faith and implementing prayers that can sustain them rather than kill them. One such prayer is found in the new book *Common Prayer: A Liturgy for Ordinary Radicals*:

> Lord of Creation,
> Create in us a new rhythm of life
> composed of hours that sustain
> rather than stress,
> of days that deliver rather than destroy,
> of time that tickles rather than tackles.[10]

Creating a new rhythm of life will require thought, prayer, and God's help. If we are stuck in old ways—old patterns of living—we must break them and establish Jesus' ways. Living out our lives in a rhythm in which we are delivered and restored as well as a pattern in which we work hard and do our best requires us to listen to the prophetic call of Jesus that life can be different. Life can be better. Each day, each week, and each month that we move in rhythm, we learn the cadence of how Jesus lived His life.

As we look more closely at the way Jesus lived His life, we see that His life becomes as valuable for us to learn from as His teachings. His way to "do" life becomes our way to live life. By accepting His offer of "the way," we find our way, a life that is far, far different from the voices of the twenty-first century, which know only three words: *busy, busy, busy.*

THE WAY JESUS "DID" HIS LIFE

Exploring His Way as Our Way

*Grace … invites us into life—a life that goes on
and on and on, world without end.*

—Romans 5:21

What if the disciples of Jesus actually saw more in Jesus' life—His way, His reactions—than they heard in His teachings or sermons? They were, after all, eyewitnesses to His life. What if we look at Jesus' life and pay attention to what He *did* as much as we pay attention to what he *said*? The way Jesus lived His life informs us how we can live ours. Following Jesus is more than following dogma or a creed. It is following a person who disclosed to His closest companions that He, in fact, was *the* way to God.

Many Christians have focused on the teachings of Jesus and the doctrine taught by Paul and lived out in the early church at the expense of neglecting the intentional decisions Jesus made about how He would live His one and only life. His deliberate choices about *how* He lived offer us the *way* we can live today. In other words, His lifestyle was just as important as His teachings. Author and theologian Eugene Peterson shared his thoughts in his book *The Jesus Way*:

> To follow Jesus implies that we enter into a way of
> life that is given character and shape and direction
> by the one who calls us.… To follow Jesus means
> that we can't separate what Jesus is saying from
> what Jesus is doing and the way he is doing it. To
> follow Jesus is as much, or maybe even more, about
> feet as it is about ears and eyes.[11]

If we want to experience the life Jesus offers, then we have to
follow with our own feet the *way* He did His life. When His ways
become our ways, then His life becomes our lives. We simply cannot
have the life without the way. Following Jesus well means implementing His ways well into our lives now.

THE LIFESTYLE OF JESUS

In the gospel accounts, we don't see Jesus scurrying around driven by
what we might call "hurry sickness." We don't sense Jesus navigating white water. We don't see Him spinning plates or trying to live
a balanced life. None of the four biographers of Jesus show Him in a
hurry—ever.

What we do see is Jesus starting His ministry at around thirty
years old. As Americans, we might think, *Why did He waste so much
time? Why didn't He start earlier? Had He begun earlier, He could have
accomplished so much more!*

For years Jesus lived the unglamorous, ordinary life of a carpenter.
He learned the ethics of hard work and a good wage. The sweat of His
Jewish brow and His physical labor shaped His body and soul and
developed in His heart a sense of right and wrong, integrity and honesty.

The waters of His baptism etched a line in the sand that marked a movement from a rather obscure life to a public platform of teaching, helping, and performing miracles. He gained a following but only after His heart and soul had been shaped by early years of work, family, and God. The convergence of Jesus' calling with His thirty years of soul-shaping experiences as a Jewish man met the cry of the world wanting and needing a savior.

One of the dilemmas that propels us into a plate-spinning, white-water kind of life is that we forget that Jesus was a Jew, not an American, Brit, or German. Our tendency is to Americanize Jesus and re-form Him into our own image. Without fully realizing what we are doing, we transfer our values to Jesus. We believe He thinks the way we do and He would act the way a good American would act. We have built an illusion about Jesus.[12]

SEEING JESUS THROUGH LUKE'S EYES

To look at the rhythms of Jesus' life, we need to read the gospel accounts differently than we usually do. We cannot just read them and use our yellow highlighters to mark the outstanding verses that seem to speak to us. We need to watch what happens in the flow of Jesus' life. We do this because we want to know both the truth and the way.

I'm going to choose one of the gospel writers, Luke, to help us understand some of the aspects of how Jesus lived with rhythm. Luke is important for us because he also became a companion of Paul's during his efforts to spread the gospel outside of Israel. He observed as Paul incorporated many of the ways of Jesus into his own teachings and lifestyle. These observations became the New Testament book the Acts of the Apostles, or simply Acts. Of the four gospel writers, only Luke was a Gentile—an outsider to the Jewish faith. He was not biased by centuries of a religion whose leaders often got bogged down in adding technicalities to what God revealed. He spoke of the poor, included Jesus' encounters with women, and gave a prominent role to the outsider in his stories.

Unlike the other gospel writers, Luke intentionally showed his readers how Jesus navigated the demands of a full life juxtaposed with the ways Jesus restored His own soul. Luke was clear in presenting a rhythm of Jesus' life that looked like this: Engage then disengage; work in the crowds but always make time to rejuvenate with time alone. Luke revealed that Jesus was not always on, He was not always available. This important lesson is key to sustaining a resilient and satisfying life. Throughout both volumes Luke wrote—the gospel of Luke and Acts—he was quick to convey how times of quiet, solitude, and prayer are essential to a rich and abundant life.

Luke wrote in the opening section of his account, "Since I myself have carefully investigated everything from the beginning, I too decided to write an orderly account for you, most excellent Theophilus, so that you may *know the certainty of the things you have been taught*" (Luke 1:3–4 NIV). Luke, more than John who wrote eloquently of rich theology and Matthew who offered a Jewish perspective, gave an "orderly account" so we can see for ourselves the way of Jesus and gain a certainty of how He lived, worked, and extended Himself to so many.

Luke's account is critical for today's busy followers of Jesus whose lives are filled with demands, competing schedules, and need. This orderly account of Luke's offers us key principles that can help us discover rhythm and live the Jesus life.

Luke carefully interviewed eyewitnesses, investigated the facts of how Jesus lived, and heard what He taught. Furthermore, we know that Luke was a trained and skilled doctor. As a doctor, Luke recorded insights about health and lifestyle issues. He was concerned with showing us how Jesus lived, not just His teachings. Luke's use of Greek is excellent, as scholars have noted, and shows that he was an expert in accurately describing the Jesus way.

Paul chose Luke to go with him on his journeys to evangelize the then known world. Unlike Matthew, Mark, and John, Luke was careful to give details anchored in fact and history. For example, he presented six different timely sources to show the actual date and time of events, as he did when he spoke of Jesus' cousin John the Baptist (Luke 3:1–2). Luke did not gloss over the details.

I would encourage you to read Luke's gospel in conjunction with this book. Journal your insights, and see if you can make some categories of Jesus' life and trace them through Luke's account. The chapters in this book on the different ways would make strong categories for rereading Luke's account with fresh eyes while trying to see our Lord's lifestyle and life-giving ways in addition to His teachings.

Luke wrote his gospel for the Gentiles, not the Jews, so he took care to explain some of the Jewish ways, such as Jesus' practice of Sabbath keeping. Luke reported that Jesus "went into the synagogue, as was his *custom* …" (Luke 4:16 NIV). The other gospel writers did not offer their readers this kind of background, because their Jewish audience would have naturally known such things. But through Luke's annotations, we learn much about Jesus' lifestyle that we can rediscover today.

THE LIFE OF JESUS ACCORDING TO LUKE

In this section I want to walk you through several occasions where Luke's gospel helps us grasp the rhythm in which Jesus lived His life.

Luke 4:38–42. Jesus had a busy day of ministry. He healed Peter's mother-in-law and many others who came to Him later in the day. Luke noted that the *"sun was setting"* (v. 40 NASB). This was a time when most people would have returned to their homes for the night, but Jesus continued working.

Luke then said that *"at daybreak,"* Jesus went out to a solitary place (v. 42 NIV). Jesus knew that something would happen in solitude that did not happen in the midst of a busy day. He both wanted and needed a change from the demands of work. He sought solitude as a change of pace, a change in perspective, a change to what was happening in and around Him. Then Luke described how the rhythm of work started again, after a time of quiet rest, contemplation, and prayer, when the "people were looking for him and when they came to where he was, they tried to keep him from leaving them" (v. 42 NIV).

Luke 5:16. This verse describes the growing popularity of Jesus. Luke mentioned "crowds" juxtaposed to the very next movement of Jesus—namely "solitude." Luke wrote, "Jesus *often withdrew* to lonely places" (NIV). The emphasis and inclusion of the word *often* are more than subtle reminders of how Jesus did His life. He was often, regularly, and consistently looking for places where He could withdraw from the crowd after a busy day of pouring out His heart through His work. Jesus knew that something happens in solitude that does not and cannot happen in the midst of a crowd. Here we see again the rhythm of Jesus' life: Pour your all into your work;

then seek rest, quiet, and solitude. Jesus knew that something would happen in His soul by disengaging from people and engaging with God—alone.

Luke 6:12–19. In this passage Luke showed a span of time that clearly revealed a rhythm in Jesus' life and work. In verse 12, we read that Jesus "*spent the night* praying to God" (NIV). An entire evening spent alone, perhaps praying for those to become His closest associates, the disciples He would pour Himself into with His message. But such a petition of prayer could not last the entire night. I wonder what else Jesus might have been doing as He "spent the night praying." Ponder this before you read on.

Did Jesus spend the time praying silently in solitude?

Did He rest while gazing up at the stars, remembering the creation by His own hands?

Did He drift in and out of sleep while talking with His Father?

Was this one of the times that Zephaniah described when he said that God would sing over Jesus? (See Zeph. 3:15–17.)

However Jesus spent the night praying, I'm quite sure that His prayers took on many forms, perhaps in various postures.

Author Madeleine L'Engle wrote these words:

> I, who live by words, am wordless when I try my words in prayer. All language turns to silence. Prayer will take my words and then reveal their emptiness … in this strange patterned time of contemplation that, in time, breaks time, breaks words, breaks me, and then in silence, leaves me healed and mended.[13]

Jesus knew the power of silence—wordless prayer—throughout His life. He knew the unparalleled energy of solitude and silence and incorporated these two shaping forces into the regular rhythm of His life. We have to simply ask ourselves this question: If the Son of God found it necessary to practice silence and solitude, who are we not to do the same?

Henri Nouwen has described Luke's timeline here as one day in the life of Jesus that involved first solitude; then community, where we share what happened in our solitude; and then work, where we give out of full hearts to a needy world. After Jesus prayed like this, Luke said that Jesus formed His own community by calling various people from assorted vocations and classes to become His followers. After He formed His community, we see Jesus entering His work, fulfilling His mission, and pouring out His heart and soul in a personal, physical, and demanding way (Luke 6:17–18). Yet the whole day began after a season of time with God. This trifold rhythm is a movement we need to consider in our lives: Be alone, be with a few, be invested in work. This healthy lifestyle rhythm provides refreshment in times of solitude. Then we share what we gained in solitude with a few others, establishing our community. But we do not keep it for ourselves. We pour our hearts into others through our work and our ministry. It's not all one or the other but a rhythm and flow of receiving then giving out, and this is a crucial part of the Jesus life. We cannot give all the time, and we should not receive all the time. We see this life-giving rhythm in Jesus' own words that we explored in the first chapter: "Come to me. Get away with me and you'll recover your life." We recover our lives by taking regular times to get away and be alone. Then we are ready to share and invest our lives once again.

Luke 9:10–12. This passage shows Jesus' intentionality about the rhythm of withdrawal. After a busy season of work and ministry, Jesus had something in mind. He wanted His group of companions to withdraw and be by themselves. They had worked hard, but then came something equally important: withdrawal, solitude, rest. It was a part of the rhythm He was shaping in them. So Jesus led them to *withdraw* "by themselves" (v. 10). The crowds of people did eventually find them, and rather than shunning the people away, Jesus was gracious and welcomed them. Yet His intent was certain: We work, then we withdraw. This consistent rhythm fosters life within us. We cannot always be "on." We cannot give, give, give without times to receive. And we cannot give what we do not have.

Luke 9:28–36. In the memorable scene of the transfiguration, Jesus took three of His companions up to a mountain to pray and be alone. What is interesting to note is that when God spoke and revealed His presence, He set apart Jesus again as the Beloved Son— the One He had chosen and delighted in. Of all the things that God could have possibly spoken in that particular moment of revelation and divine encounter, He chose to say, "*Listen to My Son!*" We are to *listen* to Jesus! Listening requires a posture of the heart and body to cease from activity and to listen to His voice. Amid the busyness of daily and weekly agendas, listening is God's priority for us. Listening happens best in a rhythm of quiet and stillness when we are "still" and invited to "know … God" (Ps. 46:10 NIV).[14]

Luke 11:1. Here we find Jesus praying in a *certain place*. Place becomes important in the spiritual journey. In his book *Landscapes of the Soul*, Robert Hamma said that certain places are known to be "thin," because in them we can see the Sacred. How true this was for

Jesus, who sought the solitude of certain places to be alone, draw near to God, and hear God's voice.

Luke 21:37–38. There is no clearer passage from Luke to show us the distinct rhythm of Jesus than this one. *Each day* Jesus was intentional about His work and teaching, yet each evening He did *not* continue His work and ministry. Jesus knew the boundaries of a healthy rhythm: Work in the day and rest in the evening. This boundary is one of the most violated rhythms today. Our rhythms are sabotaged when we bring work home and get on the computer to finish what we did not complete during the workday. We never seem to know when to stop, so we don't. A morning-evening rhythm like Jesus lived helps us know when to begin and when to cease.

Luke 22:39–40. "Jesus went out *as usual* to the Mount of Olives" (v. 39 NIV). It's Luke's reminder again of what Jesus did in Luke 5:16: "Jesus often withdrew to lonely places" (NIV). It was the norm and not the exception for Jesus to withdraw and be alone. He knew that something would happen in the alone times—the times of solitude that could not and would not happen in the crowds or even with His close companions. Note, too, that Luke said that there was a "place," a specific clearing perhaps in the olive trees that felt like home to Him, a comfortable place that was secluded, protected, and private. In that private place on this occasion Jesus agonized over what was about to happen to Him: suffering and sacrifice. The trees and the clearing in them made a safe place for Jesus to be alone, show emotion, and vent His feelings to God.

Luke was clear in showing the rhythm of Jesus' life: "As the sun was setting." "At daybreak." "Often withdrew." "Spent the night." "Listen." "Certain place." "Each day." "As usual."

These words describe the rhythm of Jesus' life. We might read right past them most of the time in search of the nugget of truth that comes from Jesus' mouth or to see what miracle He performed next. But if we pause in these words, we will begin to see how significant they were to Jesus, and then we must ask what place they have in our lives. We learn not just from the words Jesus spoke but also from the way He lived.

STORIES OF MODERN PILGRIMS

Rich and Carla graduated from a Christian college, got married, and moved to the mission field. They both had a dream of sharing Jesus with others who had never heard His teachings. But eighteen months after they arrived in their assigned country, they came back home. They left enthusiastic and invigorated. They returned broken and discouraged. Both shared that they had worked over seventy hours a week in a tireless effort with dozens of volunteer teams to build a children's center from a crumbling building. They said, "We never had a day off. We never had one moment to ourselves. We hosted college students in our homes who stayed up late playing games, and we found ourselves playing the games with them until the early-morning hours. We went to bed exhausted, got up exhausted, did our work exhausted, and fought all the time—it seemed." Rich and Carla were introduced to the lifestyle of Jesus at one of our retreats and sat there stunned. "Why has no one *ever* told us this before?" It was an epiphany—an encounter with the lifestyle of Jesus that informed them of a rhythm that had been withheld from them—despite the fact that both were graduates of a Bible school.

I understand Rich and Carla's frustration. After graduating college and grad school and pursuing a doctorate in another place of "higher learning," I realized that no teacher, professor, or preacher had ever shown me how Jesus lived His life. It was all about His teaching, correct doctrine, and church history. I grew up ignorant of the ways of Jesus.

Just yesterday two executives drove up from Colorado Springs to visit our retreat. They had reserved a room in our inn to talk and share. Yet the first thing out of both of their mouths upon arriving was "Tell me you have Wi-Fi! How do I get the password?" They were unaware of the three mountain ranges you can see from our nine-thousand-foot platform. They did not notice the quaking aspens, the gentle summer breeze, the red Indian brushes cresting the hillside ahead of them. They seemed panicked—eager to stay connected to the world, their voice mails, and the incoming emails needing their "OK" or "No." We really do not know how to be off, unwired, and untethered from the demands of the world, and yet, imagining Jesus doing just that is frankly beyond our comprehension.

YOUR LIFE NOW

I've discovered that most of us as busy Americans actually do not know how to listen to Jesus as God told us to do. Our minds are so filled with noise and our hearts are so rattled with busyness that we don't know how to be quiet, to be still—nor do we know how to really know God as the psalmist described in Psalm 46:10: "Be still, and know … God" (NIV).

I coach people to go easy on themselves and to try three things when practicing the lifestyle of Jesus.

First, choose to be quiet and still for an agreed amount of time each day. Being quiet and still is different from having your Bible study or reading the Bible through in a year. It is making the choice to get in a comfortable position and then to move to the next step.

Second, become aware of your outer and inner worlds. By "becoming aware," I mean pay attention to what is going on around you. When I do this, I write about my outer world in my journal. "It's about 80 degrees outside. Gentle breeze. Flag is flapping and a yellow-tailed hawk is circling the field." I'm simply paying attention to what is going on around me. Then I do the same for my inner world. I pay attention to my body, my heart, and my mind. "I feel anxious and I feel tired—a bad combination. I so need this time with You, Father. I wonder if I turned off the coffeepot before I came outside." I simply monitor where my mind wants to go and has already gone ahead of me. I am simply trying to clear my mind and turn down the volume knob of my heart so I might hear from God. To listen to God, I must quiet my mind as well as my heart. Let me digress a moment because many people who are learning to be quiet and still report that shortly after trying, they begin to hear voices inside that say things like "This is a waste of time." "You are *never* going to be able to do this." "Get up and do something important!" "You could have finished the report due tomorrow if you weren't out here wasting your life." The voices inside also say negative, demeaning, condemning things like "You are so messed up." "Remember what you did in college that night?" "You can't do this. This is for monks, not insurance salesmen." We need to remember that there is *no* condemnation in God's voice or in Jesus' acceptance of us. Replacing those lies by quietly saying a Scripture like "I am the beloved of God and I matter in God's eyes" can be a great help. Henri Nouwen called these voices "monkeys in the banana trees" that are squealing and fighting until you throw them a banana. It is helpful to learn how to quiet the monkeys in your head that are telling you lies instead of the truth.

Finally, just do it! Every way of life we explore in this book will simply extend for you the invitation to simply act on it. That decision is the most important one, and it is the first step to living the Jesus life. The Chinese have a saying that goes, "The journey of a thousand miles begins with the first step." The first step to living the Jesus life begins with a decision: "Today, I will spend fifteen minutes practicing this one way of Jesus. I will take a break from my work and go somewhere quiet. I will not take my phone because it will pull me back into the world I want to leave for a moment. I will sit here, and I will be still. I will do what Jesus did. I will follow His ways." This practice is how many of the spiritual fathers and mothers throughout the history of Christianity have told us to begin. In our busy culture, there is no doubt that learning to be quiet, unplugged, and silent is among the most important and most revolutionary disciplines you can implement into your life right now.

Part 3

FINDING THE WAY

THE WAY OF DAILINESS

Living the Jesus Life Every Day

*Therefore we do not lose heart. Though outwardly we are wasting
away, yet inwardly we are being renewed day by day.*

—2 Corinthians 4:16 (NIV)

Joan Chittister once said, "Dailiness, routine, sameness frees the
heart to traffic in more important matters." Branching off that idea,
living the Jesus life comes down to simply living each day well. In
the dailiness of our lives the holy meets the ordinary. Glory intersects
with ruin. The sacred meets the routine. The lifelong journey to
heaven is often marked with ordinary days where we simply do our
work and serve God the best way we believe we can. It may be in the
dailiness that we are most deeply tempted to leave our first love of
Jesus and pursue some other wild lover who lures us into believing
gratification will come in a different kind of life. The abundant life
requires a long, steady cadence in the same direction toward heaven.
Monks who fled to the desert to live out their lives wove baskets
every day to sell in order to help the poor. And if the baskets went
unsold, the monks would unbraid them and begin the process over
again—the next day—every day.

Dailiness is where we most long for our transformation—
whether it involves losing your temper with your child, speaking
curtly to someone at work, losing patience in the checkout line at

the store, arguing with your spouse then muttering words you hope he or she doesn't hear, or neglecting your prayers or Bible reading for long seasons. The ability to fast-forward music and movies tempts us to think that we can fast-forward through the parts of our lives that seem boring or too difficult to face. But we really can't.

The children of Israel wandered in the desert for forty years. Manna gathering was a daily event. Each day held the bleakness of wilderness with no exit strategy to follow. Days folded into weeks and weeks into years. Years gave way to decades and decades to a lifetime of a bewildering dailiness. We may think that such ordinary dailiness is a waste. But during these times, the children of Israel learned about God's faithfulness. They learned about their need for God. They learned about "Give us this day." The dailiness of what may at first seem mind-numbing and dry is actually fertile soil for the roots of our lives. Our daily behaviors drive these roots down deep to water we might otherwise bypass in search of some exotic oasis.

I believe our culture, not God, shapes our hope for the glamorous and sensational life. As I travel internationally with my work, I am often confronted with the lack of daily choices people face in developing countries. The bushman in the desert of Ethiopia who fervently believes in Jesus Christ with all his heart does not wonder where his family might go next weekend for fun. The poor woman making straw mats in the slums of Calcutta does not anticipate which restaurant will be the setting for dinner tomorrow night. The abundant life is not based on a plethora of options that seem exciting, life-giving, and dramatic. If this were so, then Americans above all people groups in the world would be living the abundant life, simply because we have the most choices. But as I have said, if you were to ask American Christians to use five adjectives to describe the Christian life, would you hear *abundant* often?

EXPLORING A DAILY RHYTHM

Famed author Annie Dillard has told us, "How we spend our days is, of course, how we spend our lives." We do not wait until the end—heaven—to begin to live out our newfound home in the kingdom. No, we embark on that incredible journey right here and right now. The dailiness of living is where we look for a life-giving rhythm that will sustain us. We cannot expect to reap the kind of life we want to live—or live the life Jesus told us we can live—if it does not come down to the nitty-gritty of the everyday.

Living the abundant life does not happen by limiting our thoughts about God, our prayers to God, and our attention to God to an hour on Sunday. The commitment to begin to live out our abundant lives on a daily basis means a focus and a discipline of our minds throughout the day—each day and every day. Silos in farming country are constructed to hold wheat, corn, and other grains. Each silo has its own ingredient. Yet life does not offer us silos to distinguish between the sacred and the secular. We do not get to label some days as "God days" and other ones "work days" or some days as "important" and others as "routine." The abundant life does not have a special calendar. How we live each day is how we will live the abundant life.

It is *in* the dailiness of our lives that we can be robbed of the joys within our hearts, abused by people around us who shoot off porcupine quills that stick us and ruin our days. In the dailiness of our lives, "the rubber hits the road," and we have to "try harder" to succeed at any cost, win the fight, and meet the quota. The workweek demands we complete each day's tasks. If we fall behind, we face an even more demanding load the next day. We might occasionally remember and be inspired by the fact that the Lord's mercies "are new every morning" (Lam. 3:23 NIV), but when the alarm clock goes off, our minds wake up to the list of to-dos. The day can be lost to smallness. The larger story of our faith lives can feel shredded by our need to check off the tasks on our lists.

Like the prodigal Jesus described, we can all leave home in search for what will gratify the flesh but never satisfy the soul. The dailiness of life seems to hold our hearts hostage in pursuit of something "more." The quest for more tempts us to escape the day to day. We falsely believe that life must be full of the heroic to be worth living.

THE INCARNATION VALIDATED EVERY ORDINARY LIFE

The incarnation of God helps us rethink the myth that we need more. When God became flesh, every ordinary human life was validated as sacred. The fact that God became human and spent most of His life in obscurity as a carpenter in a small village called Nazareth gives us perspective. Through the incarnation, we learn that every life has dignity and significance; every ordinary life matters. The mystery of the incarnation helps us remember that an ordinary life is, in fact, a life worth living or else God would have chosen a different life, a different town, and perhaps a more "relevant" time, like right now.

Movies may inspire us. Fiction may motivate us. Poems may stir us. But nothing on this earth can do for us what the incarnation of God in the flesh does for redeeming the ordinary life. The schoolteacher, the stay-at-home mom, the administrative assistant, the

CEO, the preacher, and the pew sitter all gain equal footing through the incarnation of God in Jesus Christ. There is no "good, better, and best" contest for us to engage in now.

Paul's message reminds us that Jesus, "having become human, … stayed human" (Phil. 2:7). Jesus' staying human can come as a relief for those of us who are born or shaped early in life to achieve, acquire, and do what cannot be done. The abundant life is a human life lived out in everyday places with normal-looking people who daily show up for their jobs then go home afterward. Paul said Jesus didn't claim special privileges. Instead our Lord "lived a selfless, obedient life and then died a selfless, obedient death" (Phil. 2:8).

We're told that every one of us comes from the clay of the earth. The earth does not have classes of clay in which some is significant while the rest is tolerated. Clay is clay, and every human life begins and ends this way. We all will return dust to dust. The world's important people do not receive special treatment in the decaying process. This equalizing process ensures that the glory is God's, not ours.

The Bible reveals that God reaches into the ordinary lives of everyday people and reshapes them. This transformation is something we cannot create through our own strength. In the Old Testament we see ordinary people like Noah, Abraham, Sarah, and the harlot Rahab become extraordinary men and women because of their relationships with God. Others like Ruth, the abandoned widow; David, a mere shepherd boy; Hosea, a man married to a prostitute; the depressed prophet Jeremiah; and the fearful Elijah also lived ordinary lives transformed to be extraordinary by God.

In the New Testament we find that the doubting Thomas, the wavering Peter, the obsessive-compulsive Martha, the murderer

Saul—renamed Paul—all reveal the evidence that God is *for* the ordinary man, the commonplace woman: the masses who live their lives in the daily humdrum of sameness. He is for the ordinary person so that He can show the extraordinary glory of His nature. Every single day of our lives is the compost for the growth of His glory to be seen through us.

The abundant life is not based on position or stature. It is not based on the heroic and epic. The abundant life is an ordinary life transformed by the power of God through Jesus Christ living in us.

Let me clarify this even further: The abundant life comes down to a daily life, not just a quality of life that awaits us in heaven. Jesus spoke to us about asking God for our "daily bread" (Matt. 6:11 NIV). He said that following Him is a daily task, as is bearing His cross "daily" (Luke 9:23 NIV).

We're told of the daily attempts of the early Christians to come together for fellowship, prayer, and teaching:

> *Every day* they continued to meet together in the temple courts. They broke bread in their homes and ate together with glad and sincere hearts, praising God and enjoying the favor of all the people. And the Lord added to their number *daily* those who were being saved. (Acts 2:46–47 NIV)

The phrase *carpe diem* is from a poem by the ancient Roman writer Horace. *Carpe* means "to pick, pluck, crop, or gather," and *diem* simply means "day." "Seize the day" is a modern translation of this phrase. Robin Williams helped make it a household phrase in the movie *Dead Poets Society*. In this brilliant film, Williams played a schoolteacher attempting to inspire young, bored students to the excitement and possibilities of each day.

Whether it was with the woman at the well, the Gerasene demoniac, or the tax collector Zacchaeus, Jesus constantly reminded people what was at stake. He simply wanted people to live before they died! His message was a rousing one: Wake up! Start living your ordinary life but in a different way!

We can wake up, start living, and foster an abundant life by engaging in some waking-up activities.

BECOMING MINDFUL OF DAILY TIME

The psalmist clearly said, "*Seven times a day* I praise you" (Ps. 119:164 NIV). He was speaking of a regular time, set aside, to draw one's heart and attention back to the larger story of God's work in the world rather than the minutia of everyday tasks. The hope and encouragement here is that seven times we would lift our heads and hearts out of our routines and toward God.

Jesus would have known this practice, and in the book of Acts we see that the early church practiced their faith daily. The practice of being mindful of the larger story of what God is up to in the world and in our hearts through a daily and systematic way is known as the daily office, the divine hours, fixed-hour praying, common prayer, and other terms.

Luke described an event where Peter and John were on their way to pray at the ninth hour, or 3:00 p.m.—"the time of prayer" (Acts 3:1 NIV). Later we read that Peter was praying at the noon hour (Acts 10:9), another fixed time of prayer, when he received a vision from God that so unsettled his beliefs that the mission of the church changed dramatically to include Gentiles as a target for the gospel.

With the spread of the gospel also came the growth of the custom to pray regularly and to organize the day in a certain rhythm around such times. This practice, which had its roots in Judaism, now morphed into the life and rhythm of the early church. The Didache was the manual used by the early church to give instructions to Gentile believers as to the practices of how to follow Jesus; it specifically taught that converts were to pray the Lord's Prayer at least three times a day. The hope was to establish a dailiness in their lives and keep them mindful of God's work—God's kingdom.

By the third century, the early church had expanded in geography and numbers but did not jettison the daily rhythm of prayer and awareness. The goal of taking Paul's words seriously to "pray without ceasing" (1 Thess. 5:17 NASB) became a goal for Christians to always live in a mindful state of God's work in the world and to sense the kingdom everywhere in and around them.

In the fifth century, a monk named Benedict sought to give some structure to the daily life of people who sought a new way of living. He established an order in which bells would ring out at prescribed times, calling the monk who was gardening, the monk who was baking bread, the monk who was washing pots and pans to simply stop and become mindful of sacred time—the larger story. Fixed-hour praying became a template that helped organize each day. Every time the bell rang, the monk moved from the task of menial work to the privilege of encountering God.

Daily office, or fixed-hour prayer, brought together the flow of physical life and work to spiritual life and work. The term *office* is rooted in the Latin word for *work*. The prayers of the monks became the primary work of their hearts along with the work of their hands.

The practice of the daily office grew out of both the Old Testament and the New Testament. Praying the Psalms, which Jesus often quoted in His teachings, is the foundation of the readings and prayers contained in each of the daily offices. The traditional fixed hours for prayer are 6:00 a.m., 9:00 a.m., noon, 3:00 p.m., 6:00 p.m., 9:00 p.m., and midnight. Through the centuries, various systems have designated the times, from Latin words that simply indicate time of day and purpose of prayer. *Vigils*, for instance, were prayed between midnight and early morning. *Lauds* signified the awakening hour. *Vespers* were prayed in the evening. Recently more contemporary language has come into use among some groups who practice the daily office: the *blessing* hour, the *illuminating* hour, or the *wisdom* hour. Christians today who practice the daily office may choose what seems doable and appropriate for them. Not many of us can practice all seven of these but may choose to be intentional about prayer times in the morning, at noon, and in the evening.

When I practice the daily office, I am always conscious that my prayers have just begun while dear friends in other time zones have already finished their morning prayers. I am reminded that I am not alone in my journey but that my friend Phil has already prayed what I am getting ready to pray. As I end my morning prayer time I know my dear friend Nan in California is just beginning her prayers. And that awareness is comforting and does, in fact, create an unbroken chain of unceasing prayer and praise to the Father. Each one of us is invited to step into this circle of praise so that God's praise is unbroken.

We benefit from a daily rhythm because it pulls us out of a narcissistic spin zone that says, "My life is about me. My time is what matters. Life is more about me than God." The discipline of having a focused time throughout the day helps us create new neuron pathways in our brains that establish new patterns of behavior. Paul's plea to young Timothy was plain:

> Exercise daily in God—no spiritual flabbiness, please! Workouts in the gymnasium are useful, but a disciplined life in God is far more so, making you fit both today and forever. You can count on this. Take it to heart. This is why we've thrown ourselves into this venture so totally. We're banking on the living God, Savior of all men and women, especially believers. (1 Tim. 4:8)

Here we learn that to be fit in life means also to be fit in the abundant life. We nourish the abundant life every time we focus, pray, and acknowledge God's presence in our lives and in the world.

We also benefit from practicing a daily rhythm because our hearts and minds become focused on God through each and every day and not just occasionally throughout the week. In practicing a daily rhythm, we are allowing God's story to shape our minds and hearts. Let's face it, culture is influencing us all so quickly that we barely recognize our lifestyles from one year to the next. Apps, smart phones, and media are shaping the way we think about news, relationships, and even faith. Every time we choose to live in a daily rhythm, we are consciously allowing the larger story of God's work in the world, instead of culture, to shape our lives. Life becomes more than tax day, payday, and vacation day. We are marked by a sense of a different time. God's time and God's kingdom become important, and this emphasis fuels the abundant life within us.

The greatest benefit for me in practicing a daily rhythm is that, in doing so, I am mindful—more mindful than any other time—that I am living my life in the rhythm of how Jesus lived His. We do not know if Jesus prayed the daily office as we know it today. But it is perfectly clear that Jesus stepped away, leaving the demands of His work and schedule and choosing to be quiet and alone in prayer to His Father. Should I do less? Every time I choose to practice a daily rhythm, I am deciding to live my life like Jesus lived His; I am deciding to live the Jesus life and foster the abundant life He promised me.

OTHER RHYTHMS GROW OUT OF DAILINESS

We know the biblical rhythm of working for six days and enjoying the seventh day as God's Sabbath. Undoubtedly Jesus observed the Sabbath, though He also understood the dangers of a legalistic interpretation.

In Jesus' day, nothing was open on the Sabbath. The sacred day influenced culture and work so they would not compete with a person's attention to God. Everyone and everything in Jewish culture stopped for one day. Jesus grew up in this Sabbath atmosphere. His young soul was shaped by a society that valued rhythm. To try to live in a rhythm contrary to what God designed would yield violence within. Jesus knew this.

Indian philosopher, cultural reformer, and spiritual leader Gandhi was right when he said, "There is more to life than increasing its speed." Jesus knew this well. Sabbath was not about catching up on what you had missed the other six days. Instead it was a full twenty-four-hour period of lingering conversations, festive meals, reflection, corrections in attitude, and encountering and experiencing God rather than rushing through life.

Today families can share a Sabbath in similar ways that rekindle their joy in each other and in God. They may even take the spirit of Sabbath into a longer time away from their usual demands. I once led a retreat where generations of men—grandfathers, fathers, and sons—came together for a time of extended Sabbath. Each day we did an activity like fly-fishing or hiking, but mealtimes became the place where the three generations would simply sit in intimate circles and tell and listen to life stories.

Perhaps in addition to a weekly Sabbath you want to take one day a month to listen to God especially well or to nourish relationships with family and friends. If you belong to a small group, you might decide to do something recreational together on a regular basis or go on an extended retreat. Look for the places in your life where you need rhythm the most. Your starting point might be to pause to read a psalm and pray at a regular time in your day, and from there you can begin to think about the weekly, monthly, quarterly, and annual rhythms of your life.

If you think you could use some help knowing how to mark the times and seasons, let me suggest you begin with observing the richness of the church year.

ANNUAL RHYTHM: UNDERSTANDING THE LITURGICAL YEAR

In my first pastorate, the church celebrated "homecoming" on the second Sunday in August every year. A succulent feast was served under the tall oaks of the church property—baked hams, pot roast, corn and green beans picked the day before, and the best cakes, pies, and brownies you can imagine. Former pastors returned to share the day. No other event in congregational life was more important than this day. I suppose it was the closest event a Baptist could participate in that might resemble the ancient feasts God's people celebrated to remember and give thanks.

The seven feasts in the Bible are rich in meaning and mark a definite rhythm of the calendar year. These feasts became holy days for people to anticipate; the people were encouraged to remember, reflect, give thanks, and grow in their awareness. The Hebrew word for *feasts* means "times which are appointed." In Leviticus 23 we learn that God orchestrated seven holy times where the people of God would come together to remember and reflect. The Israelites enjoyed the feasts as an integral part of their rhythm and flow of life. Those holy days shaped the mind and soul of every Jew who participated in them—including Jesus.

As Americans we may be shaped more in our understanding of time by observing certain holidays and historical dates: Martin Luther King's birthday, Memorial Day, Independence Day, 9/11, and more. Days marked on the annual calendar bring attention to when we might have time off from work. We might get to go skiing or have a long weekend. But the rhythm of the church year offers an opportunity to observe seasons and set aside particular days for remembering and celebrating the presence of God in our lives.

The early church adopted the Jewish pattern of regular times to celebrate, worship, and enjoy family and friends. Luke documented this for us in Acts where we see early Christians gathering on certain feast days such as Pentecost: "When the Feast of Pentecost came, they were all together in one place" (Acts 2:1). Out of the Jewish rhythm, a calendar and lifestyle developed over time to help early Christians participate in the ongoing story of God by celebrating Advent, Epiphany, Lent, Easter, Pentecost, and more.

The regular observance of the rhythm and calendar of the church became known as the liturgy. *Liturgy* comes from two Greek words: *laos*, meaning "the people," and *ergon*, meaning "to work." The "work of the people" or the liturgy is the remembrance of the times, events, and acts of God in human history. Liturgy is really the attempt to live according to a sacred time and a sacred rhythm. It is the historical church's way to follow the movement of God in life and worship.

The calendar of time lived out in the church year is where we see the two Greek words for *time* intersect: *kairos* and *chronos*. Chronos time is human time. *Kairos* is the word for God's timing in life, where God transcended human time and entered into time and space, and dramatic events happened and continue to happen. Kairos time is when Jesus was born or when God raised Him from the dead. By choosing to live in a calendar that has the order and structure of kairos as well as chronos, we are entering a story that is not based solely on the events of our lives but also on the events and chapters in God's story. Time becomes sacred, not secular. All time is in God's hands when we live in an annual rhythm. As the psalmist prayed, "My times are in your hands" (Ps. 31:15 NIV).

Through living according to what is called a liturgical calendar, you have the opportunity to view time as God views time and to see sacred seasons, not just baseball, football, and basketball. Followers of Jesus who have been shaped by the liturgical year find a profound rhythm with unparalleled meaning to the spiritual pilgrimage. By simply following the flow of the life of Jesus Christ in the course of a year, one can find a pace that is life-giving with anticipation, reflection, and meaning.

When you look at all the seasons of the church year, you are actually viewing the ebbing and flowing seasons of Jesus' life. So to follow the church year is to follow the growth, challenges, and victories of Jesus.

The church year begins with Advent, the season of waiting before the birth of Jesus—which all time centers around for Christians— and expecting that Christ will one day come again. Advent flows into Christmas, followed by Epiphany, the season that marks the arrival of the Gentile magi to worship Jesus, the reality that the gospel is for all people. *Epiphany* means "manifestation," and in this season each year, we see how Jesus revealed His true identity to His followers.

Lent begins on Ash Wednesday, when we are marked on the fore-head with ash that reminds us that we are dust and will not live forever. What a great annual reminder that stands in the face of the media, which promote youthfulness forever with no wrinkles or blemishes. In following the life of Jesus, we enter His challenges, temptations, and aloneness. Holy Week marks the week of passion or suffering of Jesus. Each day, we enter into His suffering to help shed light on our own.

And at the end of Holy Week, we once again relive the joy of God's raising Jesus from the dead and the promise that we too will be raised.

Pentecost allows us to enter the life of the church and celebrate a season of the Spirit. During this time, we ponder and reflect upon the basic teachings of Jesus and His followers in the New Testament. From here, a long season called "Ordinary Time" unfolds to help us on the step-by-step journey home to heaven. Not every season has the drama of Christmas or Easter. Many periods of life seem long and winding—ordinary. These seasons remind us of the themes of patience, endurance, long-suffering, and coping.

Jesus' life is lived out every twelve months, and we are invited to share each season of His life and allow His life to inspire, help, encourage, and minister to us. It's then repeated each year. We don't always get what we need to join in the Christian life the first time we hear Jesus' story. We need it repeated, and in doing so, we gain new insight that we missed the year before. We get to try it differently each time. We are invited to walk the journey and live it out—hopefully better than the last time. Each year is a gracious invitation to live life out again.

When we mark certain seasons and events, we do more than light candles and sing hymns. We live out the very life of Jesus by following the flow of His life from beginning to end, then we start over. Year after year, we have another chance to see what we did not see before. In each year, something may happen in our own journeys to jar us. We can then wipe the sleep from our secular eyes and see life as God intended.

A year begins in one day, and one day rolls out to a year. We find the dailiness of the Jesus life in the rhythm of the sun rising and setting each day and the earth spinning around the sun each year. Each day we can sanctify the small moments, and each year we can relive the drama of Jesus' life and ministry. Both habits anchor rhythm as essential to the Jesus life, one day at a time.

FINDING YOUR DAILY, WEEKLY, MONTHLY, AND ANNUAL RHYTHM

1. Rhythm comes down to how you intend to live your life each day. Given what you've explored in this chapter about the daily rhythm and times of prayer, how can you include time or times each day for prayer, reflection, and silence? Would you need to set aside the same time for each day? How would you like to spend your time? Karen, a stay-at-home mom, chooses the naptime of her children to go to her bedroom and use the hour to read the Bible, journal a few thoughts, and pray. She said, "This *rhythm thing* sustains me more than anything else I can do. It's time for just me—no one else. I take my mom hat off, my wife hat off, and I'm just Karen. It's the most important time I have each day."

2. Purchase a copy of a version of the daily office. I recommend Phyllis Tickle's *The Divine Hours*. There is a travel version, an online version, and a series developed for each season or quarter of the year. Try using the daily office rhythm of praying

at specific times of the day, and reflect on your thoughts. You might discover friends in different time zones who will anchor you in unceasing prayer.

3. Purchase or print a calendar for the next twelve months. Or just use your online calendar to plan ahead for personal rhythm. Mark down days that you intend to keep for your personal Sabbath. See if you can calendar one day per month for a time of personal retreat, spiritual growth, and reflection.

4. With your closest and most life-giving friends, plan a long weekend filled with fun, leisure, and the opportunity to share deeply. Trust me, if you plan well, this could easily turn into an annual event.

5. Ask your pastor or a leader in your church to consider teaching a class or series on the liturgical calendar and its benefits. Because I was not raised in a liturgical tradition, I've found it fascinating to understand the meaning of the colors used in the church, the variety of songs sung, the different prayers designated for certain seasons, and more. What's even more important is to have repeated opportunities each year to sense the rhythm of the church year and gain fresh insights.

THE WAY OF HIDDENNESS

Choosing Obscurity to Cultivate Life

Meanwhile, be content with obscurity, like Christ.

—Colossians 3:4

THE HIDDEN LIFE OF JESUS

It is stunning to realize that we know so little of Jesus' life. We have a record of a mere thirty-six months of His adult life and two brief birth narratives. Matthew and Luke gave us only a glimpse into His early life. When you compile all four gospel accounts, only four brief chapters offer any information whatsoever about the early years of Jesus' life. In those short accounts we read about His birth, and only Luke's gives us one other insight into the formative years of Jesus' life: the story of the twelve-year-old Jesus leaving His parents after a religious festival and returning alone to the temple courts where He engaged in astonishing encounters with the teachers of the Law (Luke 2:41–52).

Most of what we know about Jesus is what He did after He had already lived thirty years—well into midlife because of the shorter life expectancy in the first century AD. We base our entire faith and religion on those thirty-six months. Alicia Britt Chole wrote of these years, "When we state our desire to 'be like Jesus,' we are not referring to Jesus' anonymous years. 'I want to walk like Jesus walked and live like Jesus lived!' is generally *not* equated in our hearts with, 'I want to live 90 percent of my life in absolute obscurity!'"[15]

It makes me wonder when Jesus told the parables of the hidden treasure and the pearl of great price—unnoticed, unrecognized, unobserved perhaps—that He was talking with some personal experience on the subject (Matt. 13:44–46). As God's pearl of heaven, Jesus' worth, value, and esteem were not recognized—perhaps ever throughout His entire earthly life. However, once we awaken to His worth in our own lives, we truly know Him to be worth exceedingly more than we could ever imagine. His life motivates us to change our perspective on life, including the value of the other things that can get in the way or even take the place of the Pearl of Heaven.

Jesus is the treasure of God cloaked in human skin and sinew, veiled so that no one would or could recognize His deity. His Godness hidden. His glory obscured. His power muted. His praise silenced for decades. His life unknown, unnoticed, and unregarded. It's unthinkable. But that is what God did.

All of this helps us come to the conclusion that God is not opposed to living in anonymity or obscurity, or even enduring hidden years and decades. These times, too, are in His hands, just as the psalmist confessed (Ps. 31:15).

Jews everywhere had it wrong as they expected God's Messiah to enter our plight with pomp and circumstance. We can make the same mistake today. God's Messiah did not come in light, splendor, and power. He was born in a small remote village that was frowned upon by the elite, as if nothing good could ever come from a stinking stable in Bethlehem. They were wrong. We might be wrong as well. God chooses His way over culture's ways, His way over political ways, and even His way over established religion's ways. Jesus lived an obscure, anonymous life, and there's something in that for us to learn.

Nothing else was recorded from age twelve until Jesus showed up on the world scene at age thirty. Other than Luke's story of Jesus going to the temple, we have absolutely nothing to inform us of Jesus' times of going through puberty and learning to become a man. The records are silent on His obscure, anonymous, and hidden life.

Archaeologists have recently unearthed remains of a Jewish home in Nazareth, the town where Jesus was raised. At the time of Jesus' childhood, Nazareth most likely had only fifty homes within its four-acre plot. It was small, not well traveled, and obscure. Even later in Jesus' adult life, Nazareth was discounted as an important place.[16] Nathaniel, one of the disciples, upon being invited to go and meet Jesus, exclaimed, "Nazareth! Can anything good come from there?" (John 1:46 NIV).

Such was the early life of Jesus. Luke said, "Jesus grew in wisdom and stature, and in favor with God and man" (Luke 2:52 NIV). Jesus' spiritual formation, His growth and maturity, His living in the wonderful and immense favor of God and also of people happened with almost complete anonymity. In those hidden years, all thirty of them, the tender soul of God was shaped and formed. Such a hidden life seems like a waste in this day and age. But learning to embrace obscure seasons and hidden years yields a richness in our lives that frees us from the demands to be applauded and to be elevated to a status we may not even want because it would disrupt the quality of an anonymous life.

The fact that Jesus grew in wisdom as well as physical stature within the town limits of Nazareth can be life-giving to parents today who perhaps feel they have to expose their children to violin, trampoline, and karate lessons in order for the children to become well-rounded and "normal." I remember trying and trying to get one of our sons into the well-regarded "gifted and talented" program at his elementary school. His scores on a plethora of tests did not qualify him to gain entrance into having the best teachers, the best resources, the best of everything. We feared that he would miss out, be less than his peers. Yet now, years later, we see him rising above his peers because he paid the price of sheer work and determination to make good grades despite not going through the elite program.

A documentary that swept the world in 2010 compared the early childhood lives of four different babies raised in four different cultures around the world. All the parents loved their respective children but raised them in ways shaped by their different cultures. It appeared to me that the most contented child was the one raised in a third-world village, without electricity, television, and soccer leagues—something like Nazareth perhaps.[17]

✦

The weeks, months, and years of menial work taught Jesus responsibility. The cutting and sanding of a bench became a source of pride and accomplishment. As we know later in Jesus' life, when He was referred to as a "carpenter" (Mark 6:3), the word used meant much more than a furniture maker. Mark's word choice reveals that Jesus was a highly skilled and trained craftsman, like an engineer or perhaps a designer of fine woodworks used in public buildings.

The fruit of those long, hidden years grew in His soul like a fine leather glove fitting a hand. He learned to be Himself and own His true identity by accepting and loving Himself. Psychologist Walter Trobisch wrote, "It is an established fact that nobody is born with the ability to love himself." Trobisch continues, "Self-love is either acquired or it is non-existent."[18] Real and healthy love is never gained through accomplishment, performance, or fulfilling tasks, however great they may be. These are the lessons learned by living with anonymity instead of fame, of living in obscurity rather than trying to be in the limelight all the time.

It's interesting that human beings require the longest maturation time of all living mammals. A dog is weaned and ready to be on its own in a matter of weeks. So it is with a cat. A horse takes longer, a bear even longer; but human beings, we take years. Sociologists tell us that eighteen years of age is the normal time for some form of leaving the nest of home. Eighteen years of being formed, shaped, and instilled with values, ways, and traditions that help us through life. Our sense of identity and security is grounded in these important years, and nothing replaces them. Yet while we may feel that some of our upbringing actually malformed or hurt us, we know that true change in our transformation process does not happen quickly. Old habits and old ways die hard, and this is true in the spiritual life as well.

The ability to accept that our hidden, anonymous years are God ordained takes the pressure off. We can lay down the burden of always trying to make something happen, and we can focus on smelling the roses of today. The secret of the hidden years is allowing God to reveal our beauty, worth, and purpose in His time. And we have to remember that His time is usually not our time.

In the Jesus life, living in anonymity does not pertain to covering up shameful acts or hurtful memories. Embracing our hidden years is God's way of growing and developing His people to be like Jesus. What was good and right for Jesus is good and right for those who follow Him. We learn to accept the fact that anonymous and obscure seasons are one of God's ways of helping us live the Jesus life. Hidden spaces are sacred spaces. They should not be discounted but embraced!

OPPOSING FORCES TO LIVING IN OBSCURITY

Today's technology allows anyone to become famous. Consider these statistics:

- Today 96 percent of Generation Y has joined a social network.
- Social media has overtaken porn as the number one activity on the web.
- One out of eight couples married in the United States last year met via social media.
- The following mediums took these many years to reach 50 million users: radio (38 years), TV (13 years), Internet (4 years), iPod (3 years). Facebook added 100 million users in fewer than 9 months. iPhone applications hit 1 billion in 9 months.

- If Facebook were a country, it would be the fourth largest in the world between the United States and Indonesia.[19]

Parents in Colorado faked a flying-saucer scenario for their young son who supposedly was kidnapped by aliens. Millions of Americans were glued to their televisions to see what was going to happen.

A woman had octuplets and grabbed the next tier of fame by appearing on entertainment shows and being interviewed by some of the most respected newscasters in the world.

A glamorously dressed couple crashed a White House state dinner. Somehow they had gone through several layers of protection from the Secret Service, Marine Guards, and the White House's social secretary who managed the guest list. Within moments, this couple uploaded pictures of themselves standing next to the president of the United States and the prime minister of India.

Fifteen minutes of fame can propel a previously unknown person into book deals, television appearances, and the glamorous lifestyle of the rich and famous.

Our culture shapes us into believing that people who live anonymous, obscure lives must be missing out. If there were anything interesting in their lives, surely they would have been "discovered." The condition of being unknown—whether in athletics, music, business, politics, or even in church—seems like a total waste of one's life. Leaving a legacy of obscurity and anonymity seems so inefficient in our perpetual quest for recognition.

GRANDEUR, GREATNESS, AND GLORY

The temptation to be famous is as old as Satan's cunning entice-ment of Jesus, when he promised grandeur, greatness, and glory if Jesus would only bow to him. Matthew's account of the temptation (4:3–9) records a threefold temptation: Jesus was challenged to meet His own needs first (turn rocks into bread), perform a spectacular stunt (jump from the spire of the temple), and do something power-ful (rule over kingdoms and relish their splendor).

The temptation of grandeur, greatness, and glory is fueled by a culture bent and obsessed on exploiting the heart and exposing the soul. I live in Colorado where the regal Rocky Mountains are the pride and joy for those of us fortunate to live here. More than fifty of the peaks are over 14,000 feet in elevation. Die-hards make it their goal to climb all the "14ers." Pikes Peak, at 14,110 feet, dominates the landscape around Colorado Springs, and you can see it as soon as you leave the Denver smog to head toward our retreat. About seventy-five miles away, Mt. Princeton stands at 14,197 feet outside the cozy mountain town of Buena Vista.

The 14ers are famous. I have a T-shirt with all of their names painted on the back. But what about the mountains that are a mere 13,000 feet high? What about the ones that didn't quite make the list of mountains to be conquered? Is their glory not as great? How about us? What if we don't meet the standards, pad the resume, inflate our egos by self-promotion? Will we miss out?

I've come to realize that people are like these mountains in my state. Some are better known. Some are the objects of songs, poems, and legends. We quote pastors, authors, politicians, and athletes when they are well-known and in the news. Yet how many of these famous people could have ascended to the pinnacle of their careers and successes were it not for the other teammates, colleagues, and ordinary, not-quite-as-successful people who made it possible?

For every great athlete, there are relatives and friends who support him or her. For every best-selling recording star, there are lesser-known musicians and singers who provide backup, making the artist sound better. For every gifted leader, there is a gifted staff that works behind the scenes. There is always a vice-somebody who stands in the corner while the president gets the accolades. There is always an assistant who remains assisting rather than assuming a position with more demands, more pressure, and more running on empty.

Living in obscurity runs countercultural in a world that is hyped by the thirst for fame. Paul's words to the followers of Jesus in Rome help us here:

> So here's what I want you to do, God helping you: Take your everyday, ordinary life—your sleeping, eating, going-to-work, and walking-around life— and place it before God as an offering. Embracing what God does for you is the best thing you can do for him. Don't become so well-adjusted to your culture that you fit into it without even think- ing. Instead, fix your attention on God. You'll be changed from the inside out. Readily recognize what he wants from you, and quickly respond to it. Unlike the culture around you, always dragging you down to its level of immaturity, God brings the

best out of you, develops well-formed maturity in
you. (Rom. 12:1–2)

God works in us and is intent to develop the Jesus life—and
"well-formed maturity"—in us through the obscure times in our
lives. Our culture will shout to us and taunt us to believe that the
hidden and anonymous seasons of our lives are wasted. However, no
time is wasted in the Jesus life.

So what happens within us when we embrace obscurity?

THE HIDDEN LIFE GOD SHAPES

When we read the Bible, we meet many characters whose lives and
hearts were shaped not by the limelight or through fame and fortune
but by living out ordinary, if not hidden, lives.

Consider the years of hiddenness Joseph endured in Pharaoh's
prison (Gen. 39). Forsaken by his siblings and wrongfully accused
by the wife of a government official, Joseph was sent to prison for
years. Though gifted and popular, Joseph was incarcerated, and we
might assume that those years were wasted for him. But that was
not the case. Prison bars morphed what might have been character
flaws of arrogance and self-conceit into strength, endurance, and for-
titude—qualities that helped Joseph become a great leader. Surely in
this time, the faith of Joseph deepened and his trust was anchored in
the sovereignty of God. Joseph was later freed and reunited with the
brothers who had betrayed him, and that was when Joseph offered
one of the most important truths we can anchor our lives to in times
of unwanted hiddenness. He told his brothers, "You intended to
harm me [force me into the obscurity of a prison and even have me

killed], but God intended it for good to accomplish what is now being done, the saving of many lives" (Gen. 50:20 NIV).

Also consider Moses. Raised in a privileged status by Pharaoh's daughter, Moses knew nothing of a hidden life when he was young. Yet later as an adult, Moses committed murder, causing him to flee into obscurity. Moses was in the wilderness when he heard God's name for the very first time in the midst of the inextinguishable burning bush (Ex. 2—3). He was on the *backside* of a mountain, in a secluded place—perhaps a requirement for God to manifest His true self to Moses and to us. Without the fanfare of human companions and in the midst of nothing but wilderness and a herd of bleating sheep, the ground became holy and transforming for Moses.

Consider David when he was a young shepherd who simply wandered as the last born of his father's sons, moving his sheep from pasture to pasture to allow them to feed on the green grass while his soul feasted by still waters and in solitude. There in obscurity he wrote the most beloved poems and prayers used by lovers of God everywhere. He was inspired and imagined the lush pastures, the quiet, still waters, the healing balm of nature when he was alone. Obscurity taught David something that ruling a kingdom never could. The sweetness of his alone times shaped his heart, molded his character, and formed his thoughts. There his aloneness was assuaged by the presence of Another. His heart was touched. His soul was nourished, and he gained perspective on how life really is and needs to be. David knew what we need to know: Solitude and stillness create the pathway that leads to knowing God and knowing our true selves.

Elijah fled into the desert after a mighty feat on Mount Carmel, where he accomplished a spiritual wonder and the prophets of Baal were killed (1 Kings 18). Immediately after this act, Elijah ran for his life and entered a desert experience. Here he heard the "gentle whisper" of God that spoke to him. He did not hear this in activity, spiritual feats, the astounding works of miraculous fire, or wind and earthquakes, but in a place of obscurity.

When the apostle Paul was converted after persecuting and murdering many followers of Jesus, he went into the desert of Arabia for *three years*. In that secluded sandy desert, Paul's soul was shaped and reshaped. He emerged from this hidden time transformed and with his heart now set on a mission. Everything changed for Paul through this experience.

Stillness leads to knowledge, which reveals God. It's that simple, yet our loud and fast-moving culture would fear the stillness that makes the soul come alive and aware.

ISOLATION, WILDERNESS, AND HIDDENNESS OFFER LIFE-CHANGING LESSONS

Words such as *obscurity*, *wilderness*, and *desert* may at first conjure up unappealing meanings for us. But what we learn is that being hidden, having an extended time in wilderness, or living an obscure life can have transforming value for us. Rather than fearing such times or rejecting such seasons of life as ineffective, we can learn how utterly life altering they can be.

God uses times of what may be to us unwanted isolation to accomplish what only living in obscurity can do. God uses obscurity to shape and mold us for greater things that we are clearly not aware of in the midst of such a season.

Modern stories remind us of God's using seasons of life to shape the minds of great leaders. Nelson Mandela spent years in a South African prison and Alexander Solzhenitsyn in Russian labor camps. Their writings have influenced the thinking of thousands and helped reform governments. Their lessons were learned behind bars and in obscurity.

In the 1970s missionaries were thrown out of Ethiopia during the Communist regime. Church leaders were imprisoned and churches shut down. Yet church historians now know that the real, explosive growth of the church happened precisely in what appeared to be the darkest time. Christians began to meet in house churches, and thousands were added to their numbers. After the Communist regime fell, the church rose out of the darkness strong and massive. What appeared to be the death sentence was actually the breath of air igniting the entire country to turn to God through Jesus Christ.

In recent decades, Eugene Peterson has written dozens of books. He is a popular speaker at conferences, and his translation of the Bible into our everyday, vernacular language, *The Message*, has made him one of the most influential Christian thinkers in the world today. Yet Peterson did not always live a recognized life. He grew up in Kalispell, Montana, not in the suburbs of some sprawling megacity where fame and notoriety lie around every corner. He lived in the obscurity of the Montana wilderness. He was the son of a butcher and, as a young boy, learned his father's trade. Feeling the call into ministry, Peterson spent more than twenty years pastoring a relatively small church in Maryland. There he pastored people from cradle to grave, married couples, buried friends, and attended elder meetings.

Yet something else happened while Peterson lived his ordinary life as a pastor. He began to write out of a need to help people understand the ways of God. Being in a smaller church provided the setting to formulate his thinking, shape his language, and sense a great need for people everywhere. There the idea of translating the Bible into everyday language that real men and women speak was birthed in him. What resulted was *The Message*—one of the most popular versions of the Bible in contemporary times.

Pastors may live in obscure locations, but no pastor or public figure lives a truly anonymous life. My twenty-five years in the pastorate have seasoned my soul to learn ways of being obscure—especially when I pastored large churches in small towns where everyone seemed to know who I was. To help me find my grounding and to enjoy nature more, our family began to camp. We loved to go into national forests and get lost among the tall oaks and whispering pines. At night we knew only the fox or the hooting owl. Those experiences have become the most memorable for our sons. We all gained more in those forests than we realized at the time.

After I left the pastorate, my family moved to Colorado, where our friends and donors helped us purchase a thirty-five-acre working ranch. It was our vision to begin a small and intimate retreat in the midst of God's beautiful world, a place where people could come to do the much-needed work of the soul. The big red barn on this property was once the home to cows and llamas, pigs and goats. But our vision required this old barn to be transformed into a place to retreat. The leaders who come, some of whom are well-known and widely recognized, retreat to this barn and spill out their lives—sometimes in the wake of an affair, getting fired, being betrayed by a staff member, or the death of a dream. There in that hidden, old red barn I have seen pride melt, brokenness assuaged, betrayed hearts find one another once more, and those who felt dead when they arrived at the retreat come to life again. It truly is amazing to have witnessed the transformation of men and women.

But often I would drive home and think, *No one will ever really know what I have done today. No one will ever know who I have been with today. No one will ever see the results of my day's work.* I'd go home to my wife and not be able to share with her because of my promise of confidentiality to our guests. My work in obscurity somehow seems to cultivate a secret desire within me for people to know what I've really done. In that barn I have had to lay down my pride, crucify my smugness, and fillet open my heart of arrogance in the midst of piles of cow manure. Somehow it became appropriate and often funny for me to look around and say, "Has my life come down to this, to my workplace being a barn and my pulpit a manger?"

Anonymity is not a bad circumstance. Obscurity is not something we should run from. Isolation is not a disease. These three realities are tools of truth that God uses to shape the souls of every one of His sons and daughters.

LIFE LESSONS FROM ANONYMITY

What benefit is there in long seasons of anonymity? There is perhaps no greater list of virtues of these benefits than those from the apostle Paul when he described the fruit of the Spirit—the manifestations of the Spirit working in someone:

But what happens when we live God's way? He brings gifts into our lives, much the same way that fruit appears in an orchard—things like affection for others, exuberance about life, serenity. We develop a willingness to stick with things, a sense of compassion in the heart, and a conviction that a basic holiness permeates things and people. We find ourselves involved in loyal commitments, not needing to force our way in life, able to marshal and direct our energies wisely. (Gal. 5:22–23)

The fruit Paul listed is not instantly grown then microwaved in some kind of church-made gadget. No, this kind of fruit is cultivated by doing repeated tasks in loving relationships, guided by people in the know who are older, wiser, and more mature. An exuberance or joy about life is not instantly gained. We learn exuberance by trial and error, seasons of sadness, evaluating our regrets, and lamenting the important things we might have lost along the way. We recognize that a "basic holiness that permeates things and people" is not just a doctrinal statement we commit to memory. Seasons of serving as a vice president or a team member rather than the chair offer time for us to grow character and develop a solid integrity. They teach us to learn by watching rather than by having burnouts in our careers because we were promoted before we were really ready for the responsibility. We become our true selves in such seasons, and again, this realization runs counter to our culture, which demands we get "there" quickly.

We learn to see things differently in times of being hidden. We open ourselves up to the sacredness of other people's souls and learn to value, protect, and nourish life in every form and in every way possible. We learn loyal commitments through giving up when we should not have and letting go of something or someone when we should never have. We find that "marshaling our energies wisely" is good when we burn out too fast, fade too quickly, or give up before we reach the finish line. We learn to endure. We learn patience. We grow this sacred stuff within, and that is the righteousness the Bible speaks of.

◆

Henri Nouwen said,

> Hiddenness is an essential quality of the spiritual life. Solitude, silence, ordinary tasks, being with people without great agendas, sleeping, eating, working, playing … all of that without being different from others, that is the life that Jesus lived and the life he asks us to live.[20]

We are called not only to live by the great teachings of the Sermon on the Mount, to obey the great commandments that Jesus gave, to remember the needy, and to extend the grace and compassion of God to them. We are also called to live a hidden life, a life of obscurity.

Jesus calls us to the very life He lived in this way. In His famous Sermon on the Mount, He taught everyone to do life the way He was doing life, and He was specific and practical in how He fleshed this out. As you read the words of Jesus, circle or mark the specific areas where He encouraged living the way of anonymity:

> Be especially careful when you are trying to be good so that you don't make a performance out of it. It might be good theater, but the God who made you won't be applauding. When you do something for someone else, don't call attention to yourself. You've seen them in action, I'm sure—"playactors" I call them—treating prayer meeting and street corner alike as a stage, acting compassionate as long as someone is watching, playing to the crowds. They get applause, true, but that's all they get. When you help someone out, don't think about how it looks. Just do it—quietly and unobtrusively. That is the way your God, who conceived you in love, working behind the scenes, helps you out.
>
> And when you come before God, don't turn that into a theatrical production either. All these people making a regular show out of their prayers, hoping for stardom! Do you think God sits in a box seat?
>
> Here's what I want you to do: Find a quiet, secluded place so you won't be tempted to role-play before God. Just be there as simply and honestly as you can manage. The focus will shift from you to God, and you will begin to sense his grace.

The world is full of so-called prayer warriors who are prayer-ignorant. They're full of formulas and programs and advice, peddling techniques for getting what you want from God. Don't fall for that nonsense. This is your Father you are dealing with, and he knows better than you what you need. With a God like this loving you, you can pray very simply. (Matt. 6:1–8)

I have to admit something to you here. Reading these words endears me to Jesus. I'm drawn to Him because He nails it on the head for us. He points out how ludicrous our culture and life can be when we try to make our lives—even our spiritual lives—something to be noticed.

As a not-for-profit Christian ministry, we've applied for dozens of grants to help us in our work. While I was writing this very chapter, we were delighted to receive word from one family foundation that they are giving us a grant to help us with our retreat center! However, one of the stipulations to receiving the grant stood out to me. The foundation wants us to agree that we never reveal or share their names regarding this gift. This is what they requested:

> Please acknowledge that our participation in this project will be treated confidentially and that you will not use plaques, memorials, press releases, or any public documents to disclose our involvement. When discussing the project with third parties, we

ask that you simply refer to us as interested friends of the ministry.

LEARNING TO LIVE IN OBSCURITY

Here are some ideas to seed your thinking and help spark your creativity about establishing your own ways of learning to live with obscurity as Jesus did.

1. Do a postmortem[21] on a season of obscurity, wilderness, and anonymity that you've experienced in the past. Ask yourself the three questions following this paragraph. Journal your responses, and get together with a few of your friends, asking them to do the same; then share your experiences. See what common ground might surface among you for insights, lessons, and encouragement.
   a. What do you think God was up to in your season of obscurity?
   b. What lessons did you gain from this time?
   c. What honest feelings surfaced in this time about God, yourself, friends, and your faith?
2. A sabbatical is an extended time of being unplugged and unavailable and ceasing from your routine and normal life. It can be a week, a month, a quarter of a year, or longer. If you were to plan your own sabbatical right now, what would you see yourself doing and not doing?

Where would you be? What resources would you take with you? Could you make this happen in the next phase of your life? Why or why not?

3. Read Shelley Trebesch's *Isolation: A Place of Transformation in the Life of a Leader* with your group or class, and plan a time to share your insights and observations.

4. What are some creative ways that you can be secluded for a while? Take a week and unplug yourself from technology and people, and be alone with God. Or consider a twenty-four-hour silent retreat with a few friends, but be careful to remain totally silent during the time. At the end come together and share your insights and feelings about the experience. Try it for longer and see what happens.

5. Interview someone you know who has experienced an extended time of wilderness and anonymity. Ask the person what he or she learned. Find out what the person found valuable and what he or she regretted. What did the person learn about God after that time?

6. Read a biography of someone who has written about an experience of isolation. See what insights you can glean from the person's experience and how his or her story can inform your own.[22]

THE WAY OF FAMILY

Living the Life with Our Family and Those Closest to Us

We've known him since he was a kid. We know his brothers,
James, Justus, Jude, and Simon, and his sisters.

—Mark 6:3

Family. The word can elicit emotions of warmth and safety, dredge up feelings of isolation and abandonment, or stir up something in between. While the complexion of what it means to be a family is constantly changing, the family is God's idea and given prominence in the Ten Commandments, where we are told to honor our fathers and mothers so we will live a long time (Ex. 20:12). Family has been God's idea since the beginning of time with Adam and Eve.

No one gets to choose his or her family. I've often dreamed of growing up in an Italian family, with visions of sitting together over great meals of pasta with rich red sauce passed around a large table filled with loving brothers and sisters and a short, rotund grandmother who would kiss my cheeks and pass me extra garlic bread. But I never had a grandmother like that. I never had a family like that.

Since family is chosen for us, we spend our days and years learning not only to *love* but also, hopefully, to *like* those closest to us. At birth, we were held by hands we did not choose. We were loved by hearts possibly damaged and wounded from their own formation—from their parents, our grandparents. We learned to handle conflict from what we saw modeled before our eyes and ears. We were raised in a family where faith was valued, disdained, or ignored. Our parents or guardians either loved us well or "did the best I could," as my mother has often told me. Some of our family stories show lots of pain; others lots of love, others lots of fun. But every family story matters because every family member matters. Some of us were exposed early to travel, music, and sports, while others were fascinated by computers, machines, and building things. We are all different, and even in the same family, the stories are going to be different. We have different perspectives, different ages from which we're experiencing our families and a wide array of possible social-, economic-, political-, and religious-shaping elements.

Our stories of formation—physically, emotionally, mentally, and spiritually—hold powerful clues that reveal how we will encounter life. Some childhood experiences shape how we will later encounter, enjoy, and become established in life. Those stories are like dots we seek to connect and make sense of as we grow and mature. Each dot, connected to another, gives us a picture of our spiritual formation. I say "spiritual formation" because I believe that there are no silos in life, everything is connected, and every dot means something. In Jesus' family we see all of this at work.

JESUS' FAMILY

Ingrid Trobisch, wife of famous psychologist Walter Trobisch, wrote,

> [Jesus] was an unwanted child … an embarrass-
> ment to his parents, unexpected, and unplanned.…

> And still, there has never been a child more wanted,
> more loved by God and never a person who became
> a greater blessing to more people than Jesus.[23]

I've always loved that quote because it shows us that a well-lived and enjoyed life—a life of abundance, a life of blessing, peace, and contentment—is not reserved only for those who have ideal parents or were born into the ideal environment. While we might imagine ideal circumstances that could all contribute to a healthy and wonderful family, Jesus' own family faced many challenges that could have splintered them and wounded Jesus as a child.

Joseph, whom Matthew called a "righteous" man (Matt. 1:19 NASB), was not Jesus' biological father. We know little of his real influence and soul-shaping effect on Jesus. I would love to know more. But we are left to piece together that Joseph was a caring father who protected and provided for Mary and Jesus. We also know that Joseph, along with Mary, raised Jesus according to the practice of the Jewish faith. Jesus was circumcised. He attended synagogue and temple worship and observed the Jewish feasts. He was shaped by the rhythms of Sabbath keeping and was raised in a small town, not a major or thriving city. It can be said that Jesus was born into a "blended family," where Joseph assumed the role of father.

Matthew and Luke best described the story and accounts of Jesus' early days. Both of these writers included important though sketchy details for us to glean how the shalom life of Jesus actually began. Here's what we know.

There's little doubt that Jesus was loved and celebrated as a child. Joseph and Mary obviously loved, cared for, and protected

Jesus. To save Jesus' life, His parents fled to escape His certain death by Herod's sword when the deranged king decreed that every male child under a certain age should be executed. This quick exile and the stress surrounding it would not be what most parents would imagine for those early days of marriage, but it was the reality for this family (Matt. 2:13–18). We are told that Mary "treasured" certain events with Jesus and His spiritual formation and encounters (Luke 2:48–52 NIV). Mary and Jesus stayed well connected throughout His entire life. While dying on the cross, Jesus pleaded for His mother's care from one of the disciples. The extended family of Jesus included aunts and uncles and at least one cousin that we know of, John the Baptist.

Through Mark we learn that Jesus was not an only child. He had a real family with all the tensions one would think of when it comes to family issues. It's interesting to note that Jesus' family was a blended one with half brothers and half sisters, and one mother but two fathers—Joseph and God. Jesus was the eldest child and had four brothers and several sisters. We can only conjecture the dynamics that might have taken place within the family of Jesus: rivalry, jokes about being the favorite one, jealousy, competition, clashes, schisms, yet also support, love, affirmation, and the power of being connected in a small town like Nazareth.

God the Father pronounced the "belovedness" of Jesus at His baptism. Mark revealed that God ripped through the heavens to find Jesus standing there in the Jordan River and said—out loud for everyone to hear and witness—"You are my Son, whom I love; with you I am well pleased" (Mark 1:11 NIV). Jesus did not have to assume that He was loved. He was told. It was clear.

Luke wrote more about the early formative years of Jesus than did the other writers. He clearly pointed out that Jesus was unique at birth. Jesus was celebrated by the shepherds, sung about by angels, and revered by the magi. Mary took note, remembered, and treasured the developments surrounding Jesus' life (Luke 2:19). Luke also wrote, "And the child [Jesus] grew and became strong; he was filled with wisdom, and the grace of God was on him." He added, "Jesus grew in wisdom and stature, and in favor with God and man" (Luke 2:40, 52 NIV). Luke offered a short but important glimpse into the childhood development of the boy Jesus: well rounded socially, healthy physically, faith filled with "favor."

When Jesus became a grown man and was well into His ministry, His siblings sometimes followed Him (Mark 3:31) and sometimes thought He was a little off (Mark 3:21).[24] Even some of His own brothers did not believe in Him (John 7:3). A portion of the pain and rejection Jesus experienced in His life was not just because of the Pharisees who despised Him but also came through the hands of His own family. Mark shared that the brothers of Jesus actually once tried to take custody of Him because of their concern for His safety; perhaps they thought He was crazy and were afraid of what others would think (Mark 3:21). We can only imagine how Jesus felt to be ridiculed publically by His own blood brothers. Pain is deepest when it comes from those who know us best. We can only wonder if Jesus' early childhood, adolescence, and early manhood were the beginnings of His being "thoroughly acquainted with grief" and shaped Him to become the "man of sorrows" later in His life. Childhood games became manhood wounds.

We learn through Luke the historian that Jesus' brothers finally came around and became His followers (Acts 1:14). James was one of the few to whom Jesus appeared after the resurrection (1 Cor. 15:7). He later became an ardent pillar in the early Christian movement and is likely the author of the New Testament epistle that bears his name (see Acts 12:17; 15:13; 21:18; Gal. 1:19; 2:9; James 1:1). Jesus' other brothers remained in obscurity except for one mention by Paul where he inferred that Jesus' brothers worked as itinerant missionaries (1 Cor. 9:5).

OUR FAMILIES

The way of family with Jesus unfolds into each of our family stories. What we learn is that family matters and that just as Jesus was shaped in His own family, so we are in ours. Luke wrote, "And the child [Jesus] grew and became strong; he was filled with wisdom, and the grace of God was on him" (Luke 2:40 NIV). All parents want this for their children's development: healthy and strong to do meaningful work, wise to make good choices, and resting in the grace of God's blessing.

Brett told me the story of his loving, involved dad who intentionally invested his time and heart in Brett's childhood. His dad attended every one of his sporting events and cheered him on as if he were the greatest basketball player ever made by God. His mom also gave attention and detail to Brett's development, exposing him to music, karate lessons, and chores around the house. Brett was raised in a Christian home where he was nurtured in his love for God and in the importance of serving those less fortunate. As a result, Brett, now thirty-five years old, enjoys a sense of confidence, self-like, and developed relational abilities to be secure in his love for his wife and children. He also displays healthy boundaries for his workweek and told me plainly, "There is more to life than my job. I want my family to have what I had, so I'm not going to get on the treadmill of success and leave my wife to navigate raising our kids without me. I know better." But not all of us experience the grace that Jesus and Brett received.

When Mark and Stacey shared their story with me, they seemed clueless to the roots of Mark's anger issues and what kinds of things triggered his explosive outbursts. Mark's anger was clear as he unpacked his feelings of being abandoned by his father, who left his home for another woman when Mark was eight. Stacey was unaware that her early sexual abuse at the hands of an older cousin would impact her desire and experience of sexual intimacy today with her husband. As they told their stories, they connected the dots and began to work on the real underlying issues that needed their attention and healing.

In my own life I've taken the time and energy to explore my family story with some trusted and loving friends as well as two counselors. They have helped me connect my own dots of being raised in a home with a father who was a workaholic and a mother who was raised by a strict, circuit-riding-preacher father. My parents raised two sets of children. I have an older sister who was a second mom to me and was very nurturing and an older brother whom I didn't connected with until much later in my life. I think when I finally appeared on the scene, my mother was tired and worn out perhaps and my dad was emotionally absent. This all matters because my story, like yours, is rich and filled with layers of meaning and hundreds of dots still waiting to be connected. Because love was not verbally expressed in our home, I began to look for love outside of my family and found it through my work. My work, like my dad's work in his life, became the major voice in my life. Sadly I became an addict, because in my work, I found favor—favor that I wish I had found like Jesus did in the eyes of His Father. For me, this realization didn't come until later in life.

However we were raised, there is no exception to the fact that each one of us is "fearfully and wonderfully made" and a "marvel" in God's eyes (Ps. 139:14 NIV; Job 10:10). This is true, whether or not anyone tells us. To discover our true identity as the beloved of God is one of the most foundational rocks we can build our lives on. If we did not hear this during our formative years, we will have difficulty believing it later on as adults.[25] Family is the primary place where we receive the all-important messages that we are loved, that we have value, that we matter.

Family becomes the principal place in life that shapes us for the good. It's also the place that may wound us for life. For the rest of our lives, we will act out the good, the hard, and the bad that we all received as children. We know that 70 percent of marital issues couples seek counseling for are rooted not in the marriage but in issues formed long before they knew each other. Issues are rooted way back in our childhoods and our families of origin.[26]

Every human being is born with a heart-embedded and God-given need:

to love and be loved,
to touch and be touched,
to care and be cared for,
to know and be known,
to celebrate and to be celebrated.

We spend our lives trying to find where this can happen. Some of us discover this within our families. Others find this fulfillment within the Christian community. Many have discovered this within a twelve-step group that nurtures recovery from substance abuse. Some of us are still looking, and perhaps our intense searching actually takes us off the path that leads to a life where we can truly experience it.

Richard Rohr told the story of a nun who worked in a prison among male inmates. As Mother's Day grew near, the inmates clamored at the door of the nun's office, wanting to get cards to send their mothers. No cards on hand, the nun called the headquarters of Hallmark Cards for help. The largest greeting-card company was happy to oblige and provided hundreds of Mother's Day cards for the prisoners to send.

Thinking that the same experience would happen at Father's Day a month later, the nun secured hundreds of cards for the inmates to send to their fathers. Father's Day came and Father's Day passed. Not one of the cards was picked up by an inmate and mailed to a father.[27]

It's called the "father wound." It's a deep wound a child receives when the child does not get what he or she needed from a father. A child receives a father wound when the child does not feel loved, is not told that he or she is loved, and never hears, "You have what it takes!"

As I work with men in particular, I begin with their stories. I want to hear about their fathers, and I want them to recognize the huge shaping impact that our earthly fathers have on us. Was your dad present as you grew up? Was he distant emotionally?

When Stan told me his story, I asked him, "How many of your football games did your father attend when you were in high school?"

Stan looked down at the floor and sheepishly said, "One."

I asked, "How did that make you feel?"

Stan replied, "Mad as hell!"

I continued, "What have you done with that anger, Stan?" There began our journey together into his heart to fill his father wound with the love of God.

Many of the men I work with have never heard of the father wound, but as their stories unfold, they connect the dots to their present feelings of inadequacy, insecurity, and lack of confidence to the physical or emotional absence of a father.

All children need to be told who and what they are. Jesus' Father did not withhold this vital message from His only Son. We learn in Jesus' baptism and again at the transfiguration that God spoke to Jesus publically about the value, worth, and dignity of His Son. We should do no less with our children. We need to be told, verbally, that we are loved. Love cannot be assumed. Without being told that we are loved, we grow up wondering. That hole in our hearts will inevitably fester and develop a systemic infection in us that robs us of joy and peace. We look for things to numb the pain. Knowing we need love, we turn to anyone or anything that will love us. Some of us turn to drugs, some to alcohol, some are lured into the dark den of addiction. We're swept away in a current of sin and lose out on the life we really want to live. We lose. We lose when we are not given the most essential life-giving message—that we are loved.

WHEN FAMILIES FAIL TO DELIVER

No family is perfect, and as you have seen, Jesus' family was not an exception. Remember, we are not seeking perfection. We are seeking life, healthy and whole life, and this requires a shift of expectations on our part. We have to learn to be realistic about what really is possible and what very well may go unresolved.

When I got married, I did not realize that I would be marrying a woman with a past as rich as my own. Through the years, Gwen and I have explored our family stories with humor, tears, and soberness. One time when Gwen and I were visiting my parents, she observed many of the dynamics that I had shared with her prior, but for whatever reason during this visit, what she saw softened her heart toward me. She came to me in tears one evening as we were preparing for bed and said, "Your life is a testimony to the grace of God. I simply do not know how you came out of your past and became the wonderful man that you are today." Of course I loved her saying that to me. And she was not discounting my mistakes or failures as a husband and a father. She was simply acknowledging to me the marvel of my journey. I, like you, have been the recipient of God's grace without even knowing to ask for it. Truly "the grace of God" has been upon me, like the grace was upon Jesus. Can you trace God's grace in your family story?

Now that Gwen and I have raised our sons to be men, we have decades to look back on, layers of life to peer into and see God at work—sometimes in clear-as-day ways, other times along dark and strange paths, and then sometimes in overt and dramatic scenes. Each of our stories is a witness to God, who has been at work in our past and present and will be in our future.

✦

My family of origin could well be a case study of a family that looked good on the outside but was missing something on the inside. The fractures and fissures my siblings and I experienced in our formative years have created an unholy trinity of tension, doubt, and discord that somehow binds us together. It's called dysfunction. My sister and I often joke that the word *fun* appears right in the middle of *dysfunction*. But those of us who experience this phenomenon know all too well that we mask real pain. It's like pushing a wheelbarrow without any wheels for miles and miles. Everything is effort. It's work every time you meet for a birthday, dinner, or event. It can be exhausting and draining. It robs us of life.

I am exploring this subject here because the roots of our unhappiness, lack of peace, and emotional wounds are in our families. We can ignore this fact and pretend that "all is right with the world" and move on through the years, or we can learn to pay attention to our stories of formation and move through the wounds and pain to healing, transformation, and hope.

Carly shared with Gwen and me that she had been sexually abused one time as a child. That one episode became the major stumbling block in her marriage for fourteen years. Carly and her husband didn't have sex often, and when they did, Carly did not enjoy it—nor was she fulfilled. She said, "Sex is never pleasurable for me as it is for Ben."

As Carly shared this with us, I noticed tears streaming down Ben's face. I asked, "What is pushing your tears out?"

Ben said, "I'm just so deeply sorry that Carly's soul got damaged even if it was just one time." Ben's statement moved Carly to the point of tears. She felt heard. Known. Understood and accepted. It was a breakthrough for both of them, a step toward deeper love and acceptance.

Other wounds affect us as well. The mother wound, the brother wound, the cousin wound, the racial-bigot wound, the poverty wound, and more. This is not the place to stop and do the kind of work needed to overcome and experience transformation. What can happen here though is a birth of awareness within you that you can move beyond hurt to healing, beyond a death sentence of emotional pain to wholeness, and through a life filled with wounds to a life marked by hope. This kind of work happens with a trusted friend, a counselor, your pastor, or in a small group. It will take time, patience, love, and perhaps skill to unwrap the graveclothes of our past. I use the word *graveclothes* because of the New Testament story of Lazarus emerging alive but wrapped in graveclothes.[28]

Life is full of potential land mines that can leave us emotionally hobbled. Our great hope is this: We are not victims left to wrestle the rage within us that "because this happened to me, I cannot get over it." Spiritual transformation moves us from our victim status and forces us to do the deep work in our DNA to really change. When we change, and as we grow, life—the life promised us—is fostered within us. We can see it, reach for it, and lean into it. In family, perhaps like no other arena in life, we must "work out [our] own salvation" as Paul commanded (Phil. 2:12 NKJV). And we can. Stay with me here and you will discover some of the ways we can regain what we have lost or have never really gotten in our families.

If you've been reading this and have an aching feeling in the pit of your stomach because this material has pulled off a scab from a wound in your heart, then hang on. The way of Jesus can give us hope for our healing. God ordained that we can actually gain new family members who can be agents of hope and healing for us, who extend to us what we never received in our original families. This is what I love about God—He offers us more than one opportunity to get what we need.

GREAT BIG FAMILIES

The abundant life is available to everyone, even to those of us whose early and earthly beginnings were not the best, not the most secure, and not the most stable. God offers us opportunities to find new fathers, new mothers, new sisters, and new brothers as we move through life. We are not left alone to figure out our lives. Jesus made it perfectly clear that His true family are those who do God's will. Mark recorded the scene:

> Then Jesus' mother and brothers arrived. Standing outside, they sent someone in to call him. A crowd was sitting around him, and they told him, "Your mother and brothers are outside looking for you."
>
> "Who are my mother and my brothers?" he asked.
>
> Then he looked at those seated in a circle around him and said, "Here are my mother and my brothers! Whoever does God's will is my brother and sister and mother." (Mark 3:31–35 NIV)

A woman named Mary recently came to our retreat. She was raised in a family where her alcoholic father sexually abused her for years. As Mary has grown and worked through many issues of her past, she now refers to significant people who have loved her, accepted her, and helped her as her new father and her new mother. She says she has many fathers and mothers, sisters and brothers. She has recovered her life because other people took an interest in her and loved her. This is our hope as the greater family of God. We can be family for each other.

Folk singer Gillian Welch wrote of this experience in her song "Orphan Girl." In the opening verses, Welch described the orphan feeling she had of not being connected to a mother, a father, a sister, or a brother. There have been no ties of kinship for her to enjoy. Through meeting Jesus, however, Welch said everything changed for her. She finally found the home and family she had searched for all her life. She wrote of her hope of finally finding her family and pleaded for Jesus to be the family she desired:

> Blessed Savior …
> Be my mother my father
> My sister my brother
> I am an orphan girl.[29]

Through Jesus, we find a mother, a father, a sister, and a brother. Through Jesus and in life, our family tree converges with Him, giving us roots and a sense of belonging and being family together.

In my journey and in the journey of so many others, as we walk along the way and live out our lives, we both discover and are discovered by other people we feel a kinship with as strong—if not stronger—than the ties of blood. We become connected. We walk together, sometimes arm in arm and other times at a distance, but we are on the same path, walking in the same way, united by the same Father.

Deep down in times of life and in a family relationship with our new brothers and sisters, we sing with Gillian Welch: "Be my mother. Be my father. Be my sister, and be my brother."

We cannot do life alone. We are no longer orphans. In Jesus, we have our family.

If you're interested in creating a sense of family, gather a small group of people whom you like and feel are interested in hope and healing. Start the group not with a Bible study but with storytelling. Telling your story is one of the best ways to be known and create a sense of community. While there is definitely a time and place to open the Bible and study it, we can often hide behind the study and never really get to know each other. One of the most essential things a small group can do is put aside the agenda of a Bible study for a while and allow each group member to simply share his or her story from beginning to the present. The kind of knowing that results from this simple exercise is profound and leads to a deeper understanding of why people really are the way they are. The following paragraphs give a few hints for keeping the storytelling focused. I share these from years of listening, telling, and honoring both my story and the stories of others.

Set some ground rules. Each group member should actively listen and can ask for more information or details if appropriate, such as, "Can you put some more sentences to what you just said?" "Can you say a little more to give us a better picture of what you're telling us?" Group members should avoid trying to teach the one telling his or her story. The power is in the listening, not the fixing. When our stories are heard and valued, we feel empathy, connection, and acceptance.

Also, decide how long each person will have to share his or her story. It might be helpful to tell your story in five-year increments and avoid minor details. It's like telling your story at the five-thousand-foot perspective: close enough to see some detail but not the week-by-week episodes.

1. Have each person share his or her family story. Focus on the relationships with the parents: What did your parents do that was awesome and wonderful? What do you wish your parents would have done for or with you that they didn't?

2. When did you decide to become a follower of Jesus, a follower of the Way? What was going on in you that brought about your need for a Savior like Jesus?

3. What is a wound from your past that you still live with now and wish you didn't have to live with anymore?

4. Invite the others to ask questions for clarification, but *absolutely* no questions that are really advice, such as, Why don't you write your father a letter asking forgiveness? or Why don't you ask her out one more time? These are not honest, open

questions but thinly veiled advice. This is not the
time for that.

5. After each person finishes, ask the group, "What
did you learn about God by hearing this story?"

As we follow Jesus and His ways, we can discover that a sense
of belonging and family can emerge with others. Our new extended
families give us the opportunity to finally get what we might have
missed in our families of origin. Here in our new families, we find
the love we have most needed, and it is expressed, spoken, felt, and
freely given. We find the acceptance that we might have missed
because of some misunderstanding, different perspective, or strongly
held conviction. We find ourselves sharing the feast of life together
at a common table where we all belong and know that there is always
room for us. This is family. This is family that ushers us into life. This
is family that fosters a life we have always longed for, of belonging to
something and someone greater than ourselves. We are connected.
We are family. Each member of the family belongs, and each member
is chosen. First Thessalonians 1:4 reminds us of this: "For we know,
brothers and sisters loved by God, that he has chosen you" (NIV).

Every family is imperfect, and when we begin with this fact
in mind, we learn to let go of expectations and illusions that have
grabbed our hearts, fueled our emotions, and painted unreal images
in our minds. There is perhaps no greater demonstration of grace and
love than God seeing fit to give us another opportunity to receive
and experience what only family can give us.

THE WAY OF COMPANIONSHIP

Cultivating Friendships in Reality and Truth

But Jesus would not entrust himself to them, for he knew all people.

—Jesus (John 2:24 NIV)

It's interesting to realize that even Jesus—the very Son of God—chose and wanted friends. He intentionally chose and invested in them for the sake of His own life as well as for their benefit. While Paul, Peter, and John wrote about the "one anothers"[30] in their letters, it was Jesus who initiated these specific ways of how we enter relationships with one another. Jesus told us first to love one another, forgive one another, and pray for one another. He set the culture of how life-giving friendship works. He wanted friends. Biographer Mark presented insight into Jesus' way with friends: "Jesus went up on a mountainside and called to him those he *wanted*, and they came to him" (Mark 3:13 NIV). Jesus wanted friends and companions and did not want to live His life alone. To be wanted is to be valued. To be wanted is to be esteemed. To be wanted is to be cherished. To be wanted by Jesus was humbling, and it still is for us today.

My friend Fil told the story of being consumed with work but trying to be a good father at the same time. He took his son with him to one of the conferences he was leading. Fil noticed his five-year-old son pass by the door where he was leading some people in a workshop. He could not help but notice his son out of the corner of his eye. After his son passed by the open door the fourth time, Fil motioned for his young son to come to him. His son entered the room with a bounce in his step and said out loud so everyone could hear him, "Him *wants* me!" It's not his grammar that matters. It's his meaning that should matter to you and me.

Can we imagine this for ourselves? That Jesus wants us to come to Him and be with Him? There is no other more life-giving realization to me than this: "Him wants me." Him wants you.

THE GREATEST MYSTERY: GOD CHOOSES US

Sit with this thought for a minute: *God chooses us.*

It's likely what filled David's heart when he wrote these words:

> I look up at your macro-skies, dark and enormous,
> your handmade sky-jewelry,
> Moon and stars mounted in their settings.
> Then I look at my micro-self and wonder,
> Why do you bother with us?
> Why take a second look our way? (Ps. 8:3–4)

David's question also fills the heart of the honest follower of Jesus: *Why did You choose me? Why me out of the seven billion people on the face of the earth? Why me?*

Henri Nouwen wrote,

> Long before your parents admired you or your
> friends acknowledged your gifts or your teachers,

colleagues and employers encouraged you, you were already "chosen." The eyes of love had seen you as precious, as of infinite beauty, as of eternal value.[31]

The apostle Paul explained it this way: "Long before he laid down earth's foundations, he had us in mind, had settled on us as the focus of his love" (Eph. 1:4). An astounding combination of word choices can arrest the heart and jolt us back to life. God chose you before He chose the seven seas to exist and the mountains to rise from the slime of creation's moist mud. You were chosen before the "macro-skies" were made. You were chosen by God to be loved—not disrespected, ignored, or ridiculed.

Living a life of meaning and purpose begins on this foundational plank: We are the chosen ones. God chose me. He chose you. We should just sit with that short sentence and allow the roots to go down deep to push out the negative voices that bombard us day after day with nothing but rejection. To be chosen and wanted instills a value and a sense of worth. My life matters. I am not being over-looked. Heaven's eyes have found me. This core truth becomes the bedrock for a life that can now truly experience abundance. A person who feels rejected cannot have abundance.

Jesus chose friends, and among the many friends He chose, we humbly find ourselves. He said, "I've named you friends" (John 15:15). His choosing to invite human beings, including you and me, is simply one of the most remarkable and distinguishing truths of what it means to be both a follower and a friend of Jesus. That we could be friends with Deity is nothing but remarkable.

But sure enough, even as the voice of Jesus says, "I want you," we will hear other voices that try to convince us otherwise. Nouwen said it best:

> As I look within as well as around myself, I am overwhelmed by the dark voices telling me, "You are nothing special; you are just another person among millions; your life is just one more mouth to feed, your needs just one more problem to solve." These voices are increasingly powerful, especially in a time marked by so many broken relationships. Many children never feel really welcomed in the world. Beneath their nervous smiles, there is the question: "Am I really wanted?"[32]

To be loved by Jesus in friendship is life altering, because in this friendship we find what the heart has always most deeply longed for: to be accepted as we are yet seen for what we can become. The powers of the world try to squelch this message and distort it. It is only in the presence of the loving Lord Jesus that we find a place of being wanted, accepted, and unconditionally loved. This is life indeed in such a world that continually measures us, compares us, and makes us compete against others for a place that is insecure and temporal at best.

Imagine for a moment what it must have been like for those first few whom Jesus called into His closest circle. The initial twelve followers of Jesus had little in common. There was not a clear affinity thread to tie them together into a tight circle. Some were political zealots while others were among the hated tax collectors. Yet they were wanted. Jesus deliberately chose friends to live out His life with Him. Together they would witness and experience what the prophets had long foretold—that God would be "with us."

The simple, arresting fact of being wanted by Jesus shifts our understanding of merely living as a Christian to living as one who is cherished in a relationship with God Himself. Mark furthered the point by saying Jesus chose and wanted the companions so that "they might be *with him*" (Mark 3:14 NIV). To be wanted by Jesus is to be invited into an intimate relationship *with* Him—a relationship that fosters and nourishes life. This sacred connection is our lifeline, which changes us from being survivors to those who thrive, those who are resilient, those who live a life described by "abundance." This sense of living with Jesus also impacts our relationships with one another as mutual followers of Jesus and as mutual individuals whom Jesus both wants and desires to be with.

WITH TIME

If Jesus could not and did not experience life alone, then we need to back up and start again at how we are trying to live our lives. We cannot truly live without friends. God said from the beginning, "It is not good for the man to be alone" (Gen. 2:18 NIV). To live in a perpetual state of shallow relationships but not enjoy the fruits of authentic friendship is to live in the "not good" and settle for far less than God intended.

So in an age of snappy, brief social media, how do we develop meaningful relationships? One of the ways is to clearly tell others that we *want* them to be *with* us on the journey of life. We can have many acquaintances in life, but we do not have the heart capacity to have many deep friends. Because my work is demanding, because I give a lot of hours to listening to others, I too need a listener. I too need life-giving friends. I choose them, and I want these special friends to know how important they are to me, that I'd feel sunk without them, that I want our friendship to be life-giving and reciprocal. A reciprocal friendship is one with a life-to-life exchange, not just a drain. Many can drain us in life—especially when we try to genuinely care for them. But the key to living a life of abundance is living in tandem with people who are life-giving, who breathe life back into us when work or circumstances suck it out of us.

Just yesterday I had lunch with Jeff. But our time was more than merely having lunch. We shared our hearts. I asked Jeff, "How's the journey been since we last were together?" His reply fueled the fire for a burning conversation: "Brutal and beautiful." Over the next hour, we unpacked the events in his life and mine that had been both brutal and beautiful, and what happened was the emergence of a burning heart within me, the same thing the disciples described at that Emmaus supper when Jesus was present. They said, "Didn't we feel on fire as he conversed with us?" (Luke 24:32). Burning hearts can transform the brutal journey. When there is no burning heart experience, we are left to ourselves, and that is dangerous.

God sent His Son to show that He chooses us. Jesus is Emmanuel, "God with us." Through Jesus, God chooses to be right here with us. He transforms time between friends into burning heart time—the time when God is clearly in our midst as we talk in a coffee shop, walk together, or share a meal. The apostle Paul told the people of Athens, "He's not remote; he's near" (Acts 17:27). We are not far from Him at any moment despite the fact that we don't have the physical access to Jesus the disciples enjoyed.

LIVING IN THE BLESSING OF BEING WANTED

I've often wondered what it would have felt like to be one of the children Jesus stopped to acknowledge and bless (Luke 18:15–17). Artists have attempted to paint for themselves what I can only imagine: Jesus physically picking me up and placing me in His lap and whispering to me thoughts that could alter my ways for a lifetime.

During a retreat I read this story from Luke, which reveals that Jesus wanted to be with the children, whom the poor disciples did not have time for or see from heaven's eyes. I asked those present to imagine themselves as a child six or seven years old and what they might be wearing, perhaps based from an early elementary school picture. Then I asked them to watch Jesus point to us, one at a time, and gesture for us to come near Him. Imagine Jesus picking you up for a moment. Sense His arms drawing you closer, not pushing you away.

To listen to people's responses to this exercise is a case study in itself. Some speak of hiding from Jesus, hoping He will not notice them. Some share feelings of fear or relief when they "see" themselves being held—perhaps for the very first time. This story invites us into a reality we cannot and should not escape. Jesus wants to be near us.

The fact that His desire is so strong and so often repeated in the Bible—this God-with-us kind of deity—makes us stop to consider some important lessons. For Jesus to want to be with us means that He accepts us as we are now and does not wait for us to change before He wants to be with us. The taproot of the gospel is this: We do not have to change in order for God to love us or want to be with us. Tell this to an alcoholic who sleeps with a half-empty bottle of booze, to a bipolar young mother bringing chaos to everyone near her, to a CEO indicted for fraud and looking at years in prison. God chooses them. God chooses me, and I am one of the "them." It's staggering to let this realization alter the way we view life and God.

THE BROKEN WORLD WE LIVE IN

While all I have said in the previous section is true, this is also true: People fail us. People betray us. Every Christian circle of friends is broken somewhere and in each member present. Let me explain from Jesus' life, my life, and your life.

My fear is that we are living in an illusion of what it means to be friends today and choosing our friends out of our illusion. Thinking we are connected and refreshing our computer screens while on Facebook to see if our "friend list" has increased may foster an illusion that we are better off than we actually are. The higher the number of Facebook friends, the more secure we might feel. We form connections based on a spark of affinity or infatuation and have great expectations for the good that will come from the relationship, whatever its depth.

We forget to expect, anticipate, and assume that disappointment is going to happen. And how we handle our disappointment is just as important as navigating the fact that we have been clearly violated in some way by someone.

Jesus had no illusions about people. We learn by reading the gospel accounts of His life that He loved many people but focused on a few. His entire strategy was to invest His heart in a few people who would then impact the world around them. The few were the men and women closest to Jesus—the ones He called to be His followers and some to be His disciples, who had personal access to Him. Jesus did preach to the crowds, but it was to the few whom He poured His heart into by telling story after story.

Jesus was not indiscriminate with those He invited into friendship. He carefully chose those He wanted to journey with. Jesus was never surprised by what He encountered in the hearts of people. He knew the heart well. He said, "Out of the heart come evil thoughts—murder, adultery, sexually immorality, theft, false testimony, slander. These are what defile a person" (Matt. 15:19–20 NIV). Jesus knew that people—even those He wanted near Him—would disappoint Him. When Jesus talked about the heart and what was within the heart, He included the hearts of those closest to Him—not just the hearts of the Pharisees.

Friends will fail us. Brothers can deceive us. Sisters can disappoint us. This is a reality we must learn to accept and face in friendship. When we enter into friendship, we would do well to first realize that every person we befriend has the potential and likelihood to fail us at some time in our journeys. Every companion will cease to be with us at some point. If it happened to Jesus, it can and will happen to us.

John offered keen insight about Jesus' perspective of people:

> Now while he was in Jerusalem at the Passover Festival, many people saw the signs he was performing and believed in his name. *But Jesus would not entrust himself to them, for he knew all people.* He

did not need any testimony about mankind, for he
knew what was in each person. (John 2:23–25 NIV)

Jesus did not "entrust himself" to the people who were eager,
receptive, and willing to believe Him—at least for that day. *The
Message* puts it this way: "He knew them inside and out, knew how
untrustworthy they were. He didn't need any help in seeing right
through them." This is sobering. He chose Judas knowing full well
what was in his heart. He chose Peter knowing his capacity to deny
the truth and live in denial. He chose Thomas knowing his propen-
sity to doubt. He chose Matthew knowing his obsessions. He chose
and He chose knowingly. Those two realities shaped His heart to
build friendships based upon the truth, not upon the illusion that
these were His ideal, perfect, and long-awaited soul mates. He chose
them knowing the good along with the bad in their hearts. We can
do the same, and when we enter into friendships this way—the Jesus
way—we are not basing our friendships on the goodness of each
other but on our mutual need for Jesus. It's a different starting place
to build a friendship and to attempt to build authentic community.

Enter community knowing that no one in your group is perfect—that each of them is going to disappoint you, not show up
when you need them, not return a call when you most need to talk,
or send you a text when you really need an embrace. We fail one
another as we each fail God.

When my father died a few years ago, I flew back to North
Carolina immediately to be with my family. I had just finished the
manuscript of my book *The Lazarus Life*. It was a tender time for me
as I realized he died with the manuscript on his nightstand. Some of

the last words my father read were those that I publicly shared about our relationship and the wounds caused by his emotional absence and my inability to receive his love. Seeing the manuscript there on the nightstand beside his deathbed unraveled me. I began writhing in pain, crying tears of loss, and grieving some areas of regret. What happened next jolted me: I received a text message from a close friend in Colorado that simply said, "Sorry for your loss." I didn't need a text. I needed my friend. If ever I needed a bear hug it was then; I needed the physical presence of my friend. The text, as well intended as it was, offered me no comfort; it only doubled my pain. The message felt like a prostituted attempt to quickly and correctly make sure that my friend had checked me off his to-do list that day. I know better, but in all honesty, that was how I felt. In that moment I not only had lost my father but also was severed from a dear friend. It was grief upon grief.

You may have your own true stories of disappointment, betrayal, and being let down or abandoned by someone. In our minds, we envision friendship working one way; then life mixes with the human heart and reveals a different reality.

This is the truth, and it helps expose our illusions and often unreal expectations that we bring to relationships, small groups, community, and even church. We must remember that the truth sets us free, not our illusions. Our illusions enslave us into living in a false world. This is the world Jesus came to save us from—the world of illusions about ourselves, others, and God that hold us hostage from living the life God intends for us.

Only God's love can allow us to be chosen, wanted, and given all that is within our hearts—the good and glorious along with the ruin and sin. Jesus knows our potential and our nature, our insides as well as our outsides, and still desires to be with us.

The Jesus life is one in which we live life together knowing that in each of us is both glory and ruin. We celebrate the glory and we accept the ruin in each other's hearts, waiting—sometimes a long, long time—for transformation. We begin friendship as we are, not as we should be or want to be. We accept the ruin and pray for the glory to come within our friends and within ourselves. When we learn to live this way, we live with the sense of shalom that we need and long for. "How good and pleasant it is when God's people live together in unity" (Ps. 133:1 NIV). The "good and pleasant" is a part of the Jesus life we can have. Each of us knows the "bad and nasty" in failed relationships. But the Jesus life is a life in which we foster the "good and pleasant" in healthy relationships.

FRIENDSHIP: BEGIN WITH THE END IN MIND

How do we practice friendship the Jesus way? Begin with the end.

On the last night of Jesus' life, He gathered His few for a final meal. The mealtime was not about the food; it was a feast of life—a significant time of sharing from His heart. Jesus did this all while knowing that Judas was going to betray Him to the Jewish authorities.

Can you imagine such a dinner? Plan a party and invite your closest friends, including the ones you know full well you can't trust. Jesus suffered no illusions about people. He knew both the hearts of those who wanted to follow Him and the hearts of those who opposed Him.

Jesus reveals to us something important about friendship: Friendship and authentic community are not based on the goodness of people. Spiritual friendship is based on our common need and desperate longing for a Savior. We all need to be saved, and therein lies our common bond. We stand in true friendship from the beginning, knowing our need for forgiveness. This need will never end either. If we base friendship and community on what we believe to be our mutual goodness, then we will be deeply and irreparably disappointed. Why? Because people—no matter how good, how strong the initial impression is, how attracted we are to their charisma and charm—will fail us. Though we plead, promise, and pledge to one another, we will not meet others' expectations or even our own. We will fail one another.[33]

True friendship begins with the end in mind, and the end is simply this: People are sinners and will fail, mess up, and ruin the ties that bind us in the beginning. Sooner or later, but never without exception, relationships are violated by sin in our lives. To ignore this is to believe an illusion.

Jesus started with the end in mind when He chose His friends. He knew what was in their hearts. Knowing this, He still fully loved and embraced people and invited them into His life and mission.

If we build friendship on initial attraction and even affinity, then we are building on an unstable foundation. Someone *is* going to disappoint us—bankrupt again our hopes and dreams of a friendship we've always wanted.

Illusions do not set us free when we believe them, no matter how tightly we hold to the false truths they promise. When we understand the truth about people, we are free to fully love them by accepting both their nature to disappoint and fail us as well as their hearts that delight us and assuage our loneliness.

However, if we begin by realizing that we are sinners and we are in need of a Savior, then we can break down our illusions and learn to live in the reality Jesus embraced. When we accept the truth about our hearts and what is in them, we can be free to talk—and I mean really and finally *talk*—about what we are struggling with that we rarely tell anyone. We can speak about our jealousy. We can talk about private fears of being rejected. We do not have to hide our thoughts of being left out. We start with the truth and build on the truth from the very beginning.

My four sons are all adults and choosing their life partners. It is fascinating to wonder if they are telling their wives and girlfriends the truth about themselves. Are they showing only the good, leaving their dark sides unexplored? Are they sharing with the loves of their lives how stubborn, opinionated, strong, dominating, and short-tempered they are? I'm saying that because I have lived with these men-children for over twenty years now. I know them well. But are they being truthful in their romance of trying to win and keep the hearts of these beautiful women? Was I honest with my wife thirty years ago when we began our relationship, or was I—and am I still—trying to impress her with my goodness? Even marriage cannot last when mutual goodness, expressed beauty, and witty charm are the only things that draw us together. At some point, we are going to fail the one person we pledged never to fail. There are no exceptions to this. None!

In his remarkable book *Life Together*, German pastor Dietrich Bonhoeffer wrote about true friendship and community:

> By sheer grace, God will not permit us to live even
> for a brief period in a dream world. He does not

abandon us to those rapturous experiences and lofty moods that come over us like a dream.... Only that fellowship which faces such disillusionment, with all its unhappy and ugly aspects, begins to be what it should be in God's sight, begins to grasp in faith the promise that is given to it. The sooner this shock of disillusionment comes to an individual and to a community the better for both. A community which cannot bear and cannot survive such a crisis, which insists on keeping its illusion when it could be shattered, permanently loses in that moment the promise of Christian community. Sooner or later it will collapse. Every human wish-dream that is injected into the Christian community is a hindrance to genuine community and must be banished if genuine community is to survive. He who loves his dream of a community more than the Christian community itself becomes a destroyer of the latter.[34]

Bonhoeffer offered hard words to digest, but digest them we must in order to live in the truth. If life with friends is to be abundant, then our abundance is found in Jesus, not in each other. Our "wish-dreams" to live out life with a buddy who seems as ideal as they come is to gloss over the darkness within—a darkness that no human being is exempt from. Our mutual abundance is found in our shared realization of the great love of Jesus for us—for each of us.

We can only imagine the illusions, wish-dreams, and longings of the few who were chosen by Jesus. Finally, here was a man who said something different from the other teachers and preachers of His day. Here was a man who offered grace, mercy, and love. Here was a man they could really trust, and here was a movement worthy of their labor and passion. Perhaps we've all felt this way about something in life in the beginning: a new church that knocked us off our feet—at first; a new neighborhood with people like us in it—it seemed; a new friend whom we've known only briefly but to whom we've revealed more than we ever thought possible—and wonder why we did that.

We all long for someone who will love us and accept us as we are, warts and all. To do this, we need the grace and mercy that is found in Jesus Christ. His acceptance of us gives us the power and ability to be able to accept one another. Paul said to "accept one another, then, just as Christ accepted you" (Rom. 15:7 NIV). We learn how to accept one another after we finally allow ourselves to be accepted by Jesus Christ. We can't accept someone who fails or disappoints us until we dismantle our illusions that someone out there might be able to live up to our expectations—including the fact that we fail ourselves. Like many things in life, those expectations must die if we are ever going to be able to really live.

LIVING YOUR LIFE WITH FRIENDS OR THE LACK OF THEM

One time I was lamenting to my spiritual director, a man twenty years my senior, about my many failed attempts at friendship and establishing a sense of authentic community. He said to me words that I did not want to hear: "Steve, the older you become, the lonelier the journey will become." It was spiritual guidance I admit that

I did not want to receive. I want my "with" friends. I want my one anothers. I don't want to be alone in this uphill life. Who does?

Yet as I've sat with his words now for a couple of years, I do believe they are true. They speak to a true part of the spiritual pilgrimage that so many others have witnessed to in their writings, songs, poems, and memoirs. I could write my litany of disappointments in people for you here, but it would be too long. But what I'm learning in seeking to live the Jesus life is best expressed in the words of the old hymn "What a Friend We Have in Jesus":

> Are we weak and heavy laden, cumbered with a load of care?
> Precious Savior, still our refuge; take it to the Lord in
>   prayer.
> Do your friends despise, forsake you? Take it to the Lord in
>   prayer!
> In His arms He'll take and shield you; you will find a
>   solace there.

YOUR LIFE WITH FRIENDS

1. Write down on a piece of paper these three categories: Life-Giving Friends, Life-Draining Friends, People Who Are and Should Remain Acquaintances. Divide the people in your circle into the appropriate categories. See how this list makes you feel. Share your feelings with a group, class, or friends.

2. Reread the section "Friendship: Begin with the End in Mind," which includes the Dietrich Bonhoeffer quote about seeing people for what they really are. How can this content help you rethink your expectations about the people in your life? What myths about relationships need to be disillusioned in your heart?

3. Be intentional about creating some lingering, unstructured time with your friends. This is time to simply be with them. What sounds life-giving, fun, and exciting? Do those three adjectives describe your leisure and recreational times? Why or why not?

4. Evaluate how social media affects your quality of relationships. To what degree do your friends on Facebook and other social media outlets fill one of your needs? Is it friendship or something else?

5. When you look at your friendship circles right now, how can you foster a 25 percent improvement in the quality of your friendships in the next few months? What do you need to do? What would you like to see your friends do?

6. Ask a group of potential friends to join you in a study of this book for the next twelve weeks. See what levels of friendship are nurtured by a short-term experiment in establishing healthy community. Consider doing this online, and have an online chat each week about the chapters and themes.

THE WAY OF THE TABLE

Savoring a Sacred Mystery

Do this in remembrance of me.

—Jesus (Luke 22:19 NIV)

Jesus transformed time around a table that was laden with food into a place of encounter, connection, and epiphany. The thick wooden tables became the thin places of the soul where humanity could encounter God, connect with one another, and see life and truth as never before.

To be alive, we know that everyone has to eat and drink, but in Jesus' way of living life, the table and mealtimes became communion, not just consumption. As we see Jesus sharing life around the table, we learn that the real food is something far more than calories and carbs. We become deeply satisfied with something that is far more than bread and realize the truth of Jesus' statement: "It takes more than bread to stay alive." We stay alive and enjoy life when we learn to treat the mealtime as more than a meal.

Jesus used the table and the times for meals as a primary and important means to connect with people. Mealtimes became the place for Jesus to share much of His teachings and insights about God and life and to relax with His friends. The table became a rich metaphor, the image of a satisfying life—not just a place to eat good Mediterranean food. In Jesus' heart, the table points us to a gathering that is heavenly where we all have a place, where the table is set with plenty, and where a sense of belonging happens in the soul.

The bread, the cup—eating and drinking—became important in Jesus' mind. In fact, He told His disciples that when taking the bread and the cup to "do this in *remembrance* of me" (Luke 22:19 NIV). The word Jesus chose, *anamnesis*, "remembrance," is where we get our word *amnesia*—meaning a loss of memory. In other words, Jesus wanted this meal to be something that they never, ever forgot. The intimacy, the conversation, the fellowship, the table, and the food—all were never to be forgotten. Why? Because it's never really about the food; it's about the life around the table that matters.

JESUS, MEALS, AND TRANSFORMATION

The table creates the space for the ever-hovering Spirit to brood and foster life in our midst; life, not just full stomachs. At the table, the food becomes the medium for the message of love, acceptance, and belonging.

Each of us has a place at God's table. We are recognized, and we are missed if we are not present. Now that Gwen and I are living in our empty nest, our big, long table has empty chairs around it. Each chair was the place where Blake sat, where Jordan belonged, where Cameron showed up, and where Leighton, our youngest, felt a part of something bigger than himself. Through the years our table became the primary place where we shared our lives; we announced our triumphs, and we spilled out our agony when we failed. We lit celebratory candles when the boys made the basketball team. We passed Kleenex when they were cut and eliminated from a sport. It is where we acknowledged our births, our accomplishments, and our woes. Through good times and hard times in life, the table became the bridge that connected our boys, and now our men-children and their wives, and made them feel not like islands but as family.

As we cross over the threshold to the table, we find that we are not alone after all. We look up and are reminded that we belong—that we matter and that we are loved.

When we read the stories of Jesus' mealtimes, we see descriptions of a festive atmosphere. At one point, Jesus was even accused of being a drunkard and a party animal. Our Lord remarked, "The Son of Man came eating and drinking, and you say, 'Here is a glutton and a drunkard'" (Luke 7:34 NIV). For Jesus, it was not about the food or the drink. Food and drink just allowed Jesus to talk about things that mattered, explore subjects that were interesting, and discuss topics that needed to be covered.

Luke's gospel is full of stories of Jesus' mealtimes. Jesus ate in the home of Levi, a despised tax collector (Luke 5:27–32). We see Jesus in the home of Simon, a Pharisee, where Simon was aghast at His willingness to be touched by a sinful woman (Luke 7:36–50). In Mary and Martha's home, Jesus reminded Martha of the way she busied herself in preparation but not in presence (Luke 10:38–42). It's a key insight for us about what the real priorities should be in preparing for our own guests. Hebrews 13:2 reminds us, "Be ready with a meal or a bed when it's needed. Why, some have extended hospitality to angels without ever knowing it!"

In the home of another Pharisee, the meal was the setting of a challenging conversation where Jesus shared His most intimate thoughts on life and the challenge of what it really means to be a Jesus follower (Luke 11:37–53). During another mealtime, guests scrambled to get the best seat: the one closest to the Lord. Jesus then took this opportunity to teach about humility and the true value of not fighting for the best position (Luke 14:1–24). Time and time again, the table became Jesus' pulpit. In Zacchaeus's home, Jesus was witness to the total transformation of one of the most influential Jews in the Roman tax-collecting business (Luke 19:1–10). In mid-Eastern culture, as is the practice of many cultures today around the world, the sharing of a meal is the mark of hospitality. It's interesting that the word *hospital* appears within *hospitality*. When we are served, the service itself can become a vehicle of healing, restoration, and recovery. I also find it interesting that the word *restaurant* is rooted in the Latin word meaning "to restore." Together we find, as Jesus demonstrated, that we are restored when we experience the life that comes from God's table and God's food.

In a home in Emmaus we find the risen Jesus around another table. It was precisely here that Jesus deliberately chose to reveal Himself as resurrected Lord to His unbelieving disciples (Luke 24:13–35). Here Jesus took the bread once again, and perhaps as He broke it, the disciples' eyes moved from the bread to the nail-scarred hands, proving once and for all that He had come back to life—body and soul.

The other gospel writers told these and other stories revolving around images of food. While Jesus waited for the disciples to bring Him some lunch, He offered living water to a Samaritan woman (John 4). He fed more than five thousand people (John 6:1–15) and gave Himself as the bread of heaven (John 6:22–40). Matthew documented a story of Jesus feeding four thousand people (Matt. 15:29–39). Jesus told a parable picturing the great feast of heaven

(Matt. 22:1–14; Luke 14:15–24). And as I have already mentioned, He celebrated the Passover meal with His disciples and instructed His followers to remember Him when they repeat the meal, which we now celebrate in the Lord's Supper (Matt. 26; Mark 14; Luke 22; John 13).

Finally, and in a surprising appearance to His disciples after the resurrection, Jesus cooked breakfast over coals on the beach. In their postcrucifixion blue souls, the disciples fished—perhaps going back to something that was familiar and comforting for them after Jesus had been crucified. Jesus appeared on the shore and gave them direction about where to cast their nets. But He also did something that might seem strange—He fixed breakfast for them. He built a fire hot enough to grill fish and cook bread. When Jesus said, "Breakfast is ready!" something happened beyond fishing, boats, and water. The disciples were *with* Jesus. John 21 tells us that Jesus took the bread and gave it to the disciples, then He did the same with the fish. Jesus served His beloved friends a seaside breakfast where the discussion segued into one of the most remembered and endearing conversations recorded in the Bible between Jesus and Peter.

The morning wasn't about what they ate. It was about the fact that they found one another on that lakeshore after such tumultuous events. Food was the medium, the connecting point. For Jesus, the meal was simply the place where He could best connect with and best enjoy those who gathered at the table. Jesus used the table as the meeting place to find the heart. He pursued people by talking with them. They mattered. His dialogue with people who had been long ignored and marginalized validated them and offered them significance.

AMNESIA IN THE TWENTY-FIRST CENTURY

Today there is a troubling sort of amnesia that has become systemic in our culture. We've forgotten the value of the table and embraced the "fast-food nation."

> Americans now spend more money on fast food than on higher education, personal computers, computer software, or new cars. They spend more on fast food than on movies, books, magazines, news-papers, videos, and recorded music—combined.
>
> On any given day in the United States, about one-quarter of the adult population visits a fast-food restaurant.[35]

David and Susan came to our retreat, as people often do, with a problem. They were tired and teetering on burnout. As my wife and I listened to their stories, we heard the pilgrimage of two people who were both products of dysfunctional homes. David's early formation consisted of regular beatings from his father and a mother who was an alcoholic. Susan's workaholic father provided the means for life but not the heartfelt connection she needed. Her mother poured herself into the local church with Bible studies, vacation Bible school, and caring for the sick. Susan said she had mostly raised herself.

When I explored the place of the family table in David's and Susan's childhood homes, both said there simply wasn't one. Meals were merely necessary feeding times to get on to the next thing. David and Susan brought that same value into their marriage. They rarely had dinner together. David was accustomed to coming home late, and Susan said she "kind of grazed" her way into the kitchen, grabbing a slice of cheese here and a couple of celery sticks there. The lack of a shared mealtime became a key place for us to do some work with this couple. Their amnesia about the table became a major reason for the space that had grown between them in their marriage. Upon seeing this new yet very old way of life, David and Susan made a commitment to become more intentional about their mealtimes. They decided that they would share in a mealtime or table-time together a minimum of three times a week. After their long days of work, now they would meet in the kitchen, engage in the preparation of the evening meal together, and begin to talk and reconnect. They would transform what was modeled for them into a healthier way to do life together. The mealtime became the bridge they could walk across, leaving the islands of their respective work and worlds and at last find each other again.

How we eat along with *what* we eat joined with *where* we eat affects our quality of life. When we give up eating together, we neglect much more than food. The table is how we find one another. It is the primary place where we learn to be joined in heart and soul as well as become physically close to one another. When we jettison sharing a meal around the table, we set up ourselves, our children, and even our nation to be at risk.

FAST-FOOD CULTURE

Drive down any major street in America and notice the rows of taco shops, pizza places, drive-ins, and dives that feed the sons and daughters of our country every day. Truly we are a fast-food culture. Eric

Schlosser's book *Fast Food Nation* tells us, "What we eat has changed more in the last forty years than in the previous forty thousand."[36]

Days in and nights out, we are leaving our homes to grab something to eat, and by doing so, we are losing something very important—perhaps all-important. When a parent tosses french fries to the hungry kids in the backseat on the way to the next music lesson or soccer game, we can hardly call this a family meal. We are losing one another. Our lifestyles force us to grab and go. We do not have time to share in the growing of our food so we buy it ready-made. At the end of the day we're too spent to fix a nourishing, healthy meal, so we buy the convenient packages without reading the labels to see what is really in them. Our schedules are so jammed each night that we can't find time to eat together. We're fragmented. We're unhealthy and overweight. We're too tired to really care.

The New Yorker has proclaimed that Americans are in the midst of a "national eating disorder." Our disorder is more serious than merely not eating our peas and carrots. Something fundamental is happening. In her remarkable book *The Spirit of Food*, Leslie Fields stated,

> If we follow the news, the best-selling books, the latest diet trend, the debates and exposés of our national food practices and production, we can feel overwhelmed. Guilty. The table we stand before is no longer a banquet table offering sustenance; it's a minefield threatening our own destruction or the destruction of the planet. With our plate in hand, our stomachs rumbling and our well-informed

minds on alert, we survey the offerings as we walk the length of the table: that appetizer is full of trans fat; that plate of fruit is bathed in pesticides; that salad exploits migrant workers; that noodle casserole is nutritionally bankrupt; that stroganoff comes from abused animals. We are paralyzed. What do we choose? How do we eat? How do we respond as people of faith? And if we make all the right choices, will good food rightly procured and produced then save us?[37]

Since the days of Adam and Eve, we have been fulfilling God's mandate about working, eating, and living (Gen. 1:27–31).[38] We are the ones told to "be responsible" in how we are living. But somehow, in time and through time and for the lack of time, we have given up our responsibility in God's mandate and lost what God intended for us to receive through meal-making and life-making. By rethinking what we've given up, we can reclaim what we've lost.

Food is a gift from God. Genesis tells us that God created the earth in such a way that it naturally provides food for us. When we receive food this way, it connects us to God. Why is it that we bow to give thanks before a meal but we don't follow this ritual for other tasks such as bathing, going to work, preparing to come home after work, or exercising? Embedded in our consciousness is the idea that food has a sacramental nature. Either by partaking of it or fasting from it, food has a pivotal role in our lives. Jesus instructed His followers to pray for their "daily bread," and ever since then, we've been doing it.

For the followers of the Way, we see the mealtime as a prototype, a sort of practice meal that reminds us of the great feast that awaits us in heaven. Biblical writers chose the metaphor of food to help us envision a feast of life that God invites us to enjoy. That feast is what we rehearse for today. We do this by setting the table, preparing the ingredients, and serving and being served—all images that converge in a powerful way to tell us that we belong at the table. A place is prepared for us there. We are wanted.

A dear friend of mine is a Benedictine monk and lives alone. She chooses to always set her table for two—reminding her of the presence of Jesus at her table. Another family has shared with me that they set an extra place at their table to symbolize the presence of Jesus around their family gathering.

EAT TOGETHER AND STAY TOGETHER

It's a proven fact: The family that eats together stays together! Research has now shown that families who enjoy at least five family meals together each week are insulated against specific threats to the family. Teenagers who do not enjoy at least three family meals per week are:

- three and a half times likelier to have abused prescription drugs,
- three and a half times likelier to have used an illegal drug other than marijuana or prescription drugs,
- three times likelier to have used marijuana,
- more than two and a half times likelier to have used tobacco, and

- one and a half times likelier to have used alcohol.

The relationship between family dinners and substance abuse is astounding. Consider these statistics:

- Compared to those in the same age group who have frequent family dinners, twelve- and thirteen-year-olds who have infrequent family differs are six times likelier to use marijuana, more than four and a half times likelier to use tobacco, and more than two and a half times likelier to use alcohol.
- Compared to those in the same age group who have frequent family dinners, fourteen- and fifteen-year-olds who have infrequent family dinners are three times likelier to use marijuana and two and a half times likelier to use tobacco.
- Compared to those in the same age group who have frequent family dinners, sixteen- and seventeen-year-olds who have infrequent family dinners are more than twice as likely to use marijuana and almost twice as likely to use tobacco.[39]

Frequent family dining is connected with lower rates of teen smoking, drinking, illegal drug use, and prescription drug use. When children are overscheduled and parents are consumed with work, the results are alarming.

The Council of Economic Advisers to the President reported, "The largest federally funded study of American teenagers found a strong association between regular family meals (five or more dinners per week with a parent) and academic success, psychological adjustment, and lower rates of alcohol use, drug use, early sexual behavior, and suicidal risk."[40]

In addition to the social and psychological benefits, the research shows that children ages nine to fourteen who have regular dinners with their parents "have more healthful dietary patterns, including more fruits and vegetables, less saturated and trans fat, fewer fried foods and sodas, and more vitamins and other micronutrients."[41] More and more research is showing that family meals also may be one of the most important protective factors in preventing childhood obesity. A study by The Ohio State University found that "pre-school aged children are likely to have a lower risk of obesity if they engage regularly in one or more of ... specific household routines," and the first routine mentioned was eating dinner together as a family.[42]

We are not talking about becoming the perfect Norman Rockwell kind of family—such families don't exist. We are talking about rethinking the way you live and making intentional choices to improve. We are talking about improvement, not perfection. As I mentioned in chapter 1, I often recommend people to try to make a 25 percent improvement, to go from a D letter grade to a B, in the area of life in question.

What letter grade would you give your mealtime?

What would a 25 percent improvement look like for you?

What specific and intentional choices can you make now that will help ensure growth and development in the way you have your mealtimes?

I've shared in another book about the deepest memory I have of my father when we would have breakfast together. We'd each pour a bowl of cornflakes and sit at the same table, but my father's mind would wander beyond our kitchen while I was in his presence. I called it "the Cereal Stare." It was a stare that I can easily picture even now in my mind. He emotionally left the breakfast table and was evidently chewing on the day's concerns at work. I wrote, "The Cereal Stare. The look that would overtake the father's eyes as his mind wandered to another country—a place of work deadlines, problems with a colleague, a crisis that had claimed his mind and heart, possibly even unfulfilled hopes and dreams. The father sat in this stare while the young boy [me] looked on, always an arm's length away but never invited into this distant land."[43] He rarely asked me a question. We discussed no topic. We would just sit and eat in silence. Now I realize the pain I was in—wanting so badly to connect to my dad, to be seen, to be noticed, to be loved by him. And I can also imagine the pain that perhaps choked his words: paying for college for my two older siblings, a conflict with an associate at work, trying to remember if he had actually returned a call that came in at closing time yesterday. Did he sit in silence because of a fight he had with my mom and felt at a loss as to how to make it right with her before he left for work?

It's uncanny how many people comment to me about the Cereal Stare, saying it was so descriptive of their families. We simply must learn to do more than eat cornflakes together and call it a family meal.

ASK GOOD QUESTIONS OVER A MEAL

If the food is the medium we use to finally sit together, how can we then courageously move to have conversations that are life-giving, informative, and wholesome—nourishing to the heart as well as the body? Remember, during mealtimes Jesus engaged those around Him in good conversation. The talking nourished them as much as the food they ate.

A friend of mine had a small book full of nothing but icebreaker questions. Several times a week, he'd reach for the book and ask a question to start some kind of conversation with his family. We need to ask more than "Did you have a good day?" or "How was school?"

Ancient monastics used a daily exercise that some may find helpful in starting meaningful conversations at the table. They would simply ask a couple of questions: "Where in my day did I experience a sense of God's presence in my life?" and "Where in my day did I feel a sense of being isolated from God?"[44] The idea was that the listening monks would learn the consoling ways of God by pondering the talking monk's experiences.

One of my friends told me his icebreaker tool was a box full of questions printed on little cards, and each night at dinner he would pick a card's question to prompt discussion. Family members could all choose to skip a question by putting the card at the back of the box, but usually the little cards sparked great conversation around the table.

David and Margaret have six small children. The evening meal is the only time that all eight of the family members sit together each day. They have chosen to light a candle and ask one question to get a conversation going: "Who would like to share about something they are thankful for and why?"

John and Denise have intentionally chosen to build into their children good memories of family dinners. Gwen and I were invited over to share in the weekly "Sabbath supper." Denise, determined to fix healthy meals, asked us to walk through the garden where she had harvested the carrots, beets, and cabbage that were now simmering in natural juices on her stove. As we gathered at the table, John had each of us share a "good thing" that had happened to us in the day. It took a while for us to go around the table to hear of the individual good things that had happened in the lives of each person present. Hunter shared how he found earthworms he could use to fish on Saturday in the creek behind their house. Sabrina's good thing was finding her doll's clothes so she could change them, because the doll had accidentally gotten muddy. I shared my joy and delight that they had invited Gwen and me for Sabbath supper that night; we were included in this marvelous family, and it would be a memory that would last a lifetime.

Conversation matters, because when we are invited to participate in a conversation, we realize *we* matter. We are being asked questions. Someone actually wants to know what we think. In a conversation, others acknowledge us through eye contact, verbal tones, and hand gestures. Through questions and dialogue we can reveal our deepest feelings, private opinions, and precarious positions. In the preceding chapter I told the story of my friend's response when I asked him how his week was and he said, "Brutal and beautiful." This might be a good way to try to get your family to share by simply asking, "What in your week has been brutal? What's been beautiful?" Or use your own questions to invite your family to share together.

Nearly every week, I have lunch with one of several friends. But we do far more than eat food. We will talk *over* food. We connect and find each other and share time, space, and our hearts. I meet with Craig every two weeks over breakfast, Kevin twice a month during lunchtime. Michael and I try to meet the first Thursday of each month at a little restaurant halfway between my home and his in Denver. When I meet with these friends, our gatherings always start with food and drink; then we start talking. I will ask some questions and they will ask some questions. Usually the conversations are life-giving and meaningful. Through our times we have built trust and safety with each other. It is a place where we can speak both truth and grace to one another and be the better for it. As we meet through the months and years, we are building and nurturing heart-to-heart connections where we are known, loved, and accepted.

CONNECTED AT THE TABLE, CONNECTED IN LIFE

Connected is the word researchers often use to define a "closeness to mother and/or father, perceived caring by mother and/or father and feeling understood, loved, wanted and paid attention to by family members."[45] And the table serves as the most fundamental tool to help a family connect and stay together.

One way to become intentional about living the Jesus life is to become more intentional about what happens around the table with family and friends. The table becomes the place not only where chairs are pulled up, whether they are high chairs, wheelchairs, or metal chairs, but also where we meet face-to-face to hear about the events of each other's days. Everyone is at the same level. We meet each other's eyes. When we look past the bowl of pinto beans and across the table, we can finally see each other as we really are. What made us come alive today? What made us sad? What made us experience joy?

A text message can inform you of a loved one's whereabouts, but the table will never be replaced as *the* primary place to really see, really know, and really sense what is happening in the lives of the ones who sit in the dinner chairs. Henri Nouwen said, "Much more happens at a meal than satisfying hunger and quenching thirst. Around the table we become family, friends and community, yes, a body."[46] A simple table with even a simple meal becomes a sacred setting where hearts are found and souls are touched—day after day and year after year. Each person's face is the focal point. We interact here. We are encouraged to simply show up and talk. This is the touch we need to stay alive and move from surviving to thriving. Nouwen continued,

> The table is one of the most intimate places in our lives. It is there that we give ourselves to one another. When we say, "Take some more, let me serve you another plate, let me pour you another glass, don't be shy, enjoy it," we say a lot more than our words express. We invite our friends to become part of our lives. We want them to be nurtured by the same food and drink that nurtures us.[47]

In her beautiful book *Keeping the Feast*, author Paula Butturini wrote about the role of food and cooking in her efforts to help restore her husband to health. Here is her extended description of preparing and the enjoying the meals:

> So tonight and all the other nights when I may be tired, without appetite, or simply not in the mood

to produce even a simple meal, I shall will myself to do it anyway. I will root around the bottom of our refrigerator, check the vegetables stored on our balcony, open our tiny pantry, and find something to restore my energy and my mood.

John [her husband] and Julia [her daughter] will set the table and I will fly about the kitchen, chopping a few garlic cloves and a handful of fragrant flat-leaf parsley. If I am lucky, I may find a package of De Cecco spaghetti in the pantry, and a bit of frozen chicken broth that I made a few weeks ago. I may find a can of sweet New England clams that my father has carried across the Atlantic for just such emergency meals. I know there is always a bottle of good, green-gold olive oil on the shelf near the stove, and bottle of dry vermouth in the old cabinet I bought in Rome.

Tonight I will set a huge kettle of water on our tiny stove's biggest burner. By the time the water reaches a rolling boil, I will have sautéed the chopped garlic and a tiny, hot *peperoncino rosso* in a few spoonfuls of olive oil until the garlic just starts to sizzle. I will have added the vermouth and clam broth and chicken broth to the pan, then boiled it down until it has reduced by half. I will cook the spaghetti in the roiling, salted water for just under eight minutes, then heat the clams themselves for a minute or less to keep them tender and juicy. I will drain the pasta the moment it is done and tip it into a well-heated serving bowl with a tablespoon of soft butter. I will add the clams and their sauce and, finally, a handful of chopped parsley.

I will rush the bowl to the dining room and then John and Julia and I, suddenly hungry from the sweetly pungent smell of garlic and clam broth coming from the kitchen, will sit down to eat. The three of us will be quiet for a moment or two as we twirl our spaghetti into the first neat forkfuls that we lift to our mouths. We will chew that first bite hungrily and perhaps, if I have hit all the measurements right, give a tiny sigh of delight. Then, already heartened, we will start to talk and laugh and eat in earnest, keeping the feast that we are meant to keep, the feast that is our life.[48]

That's it—"the feast that is our life." A meal becomes more than a meal. Time becomes more than the passing of the chronological minutes. Jesus invited those He encountered to a meal that would be transformed to a feast, which would become their very lives. We can do the same, and by doing so, we are not only living the Jesus life ourselves but also inviting others to join in the feast.

SUGGESTIONS FOR FEASTING

1. Invite a friend over and plan a menu together. Instead of having everything ready to eat, do the

preparation together. Let the whole time of preparing and cooking the meal become a part of the experience. Could you see yourself doing this regularly? With a small group? With your neighbors on an occasional basis?

2. Try to have table-time over a meal with family or friends three times a week as a minimum—more if you can. Do this for a month, then see what you notice.

3. As you practice this way, remember that it's not about the actual food or the way it is served. It is about the sense of belonging together, nurturing, and sharing that is most important. By keeping the menu simple, you'll avoid the stress of worrying about the budget and complexity of the preparation.

4. Consider a "soup on Monday" menu where you can prepare a simple soup and invite someone you'd like to get to know better. By having it down on your calendar and planning to do this with some regularity, you'll be able to plan ahead, thus lowering the stress of preparation.

5. How can you foster a good conversation around your table meal? Consider a site such as www.conversationstarters.com/101.htm as a possible resource for good questions to use for family or guests.

THE WAY OF DOING GOOD

Extending Life to Others

God anointed Jesus of Nazareth with the Holy Spirit
and power, and … he went around doing good.

—Acts 10:38 (NIV)

We read in the book of Acts that Jesus went around "doing good." Nearly every scholar who has ever written about Jesus, whether believer or skeptic, agrees on this one thing—Jesus was a man who did good things. A simple reading of any of the Gospels reveals this. There's an important clue here for us in search of how to live our lives. As followers of Jesus, we also are to do good things (Acts 10:38). Doing good to others is an important part of living a meaningful, satisfying, and abundant life. A good life is one that is involved in doing good things, serving others, and loving people well.

Life may be simpler than we've ever realized. We don't need twenty-one laws, seven habits, or fourteen principles to guide us in life's purpose or mission statement. To simply do good may well be what God intended for each one of us. Many of us have so much baggage from our pasts that instructs us what we have to do to be a good Christian. Some of that baggage can be tossed out when we realize the utter simplicity in Jesus' life. The ease of living a meaningful life can be refreshing when we embrace this simple and too-often-neglected way. It's stunning to sit with that short sentence that summarizes the life of Jesus: "He went around doing good." It seems so simple and perhaps even ineffective in today's culture to have one's life reduced to such a statement.

Jesus' one solitary life impacted the world for centuries because of the good He did. The oft-quoted essay "One Solitary Life" by James Allan Francis describes the life of Jesus this way:

> He was born in an obscure village
> The child of a peasant woman
> He grew up in another obscure village
> Where he worked in a carpenter shop
> Until he was thirty
>
> He never wrote a book
> He never held an office
> He never went to college
> He never visited a big city
> He never travelled more than two hundred miles
> From the place where he was born
> He did none of the things
> Usually associated with greatness
> He had no credentials but himself.

The power of doing good with one's life is exemplified in the very life of Jesus; no one compares to His greatness or has had His influence. Francis concluded his poem this way:

> Nineteen [now twenty-one] centuries have come and gone

And today Jesus is the central figure of the human race
And the leader of mankind's progress
All the armies that have ever marched
All the navies that have ever sailed
All the parliaments that have ever sat
All the kings that ever reigned put together
Have not affected the life of mankind on earth
As powerfully as that one solitary life.[49]

Jesus did good. He served others, and He loved well.

- To women, who were treated like possessions, Jesus did good in offering them dignity and recognition.
- To the poor, He did good by reminding them of their value and worth in God's eyes.
- To the sick, He did good by healing them.
- To those trapped by the bars of religion, human effort, and ignoble trying, He did good in offering them freedom from trying and offered them a relationship with God through love, not strain and achievement.
- To the outsiders, He did good in making them feel like they were on the inside.
- To the disenfranchised, He did good by offering them residency in the kingdom of God.
- To the overlooked and ignored, He did good by showing them their place and reassuring them that they belonged.

The apostle John wrote in his biography of Jesus that "there are so many other *things* Jesus did. If they were all written down, each of them, one by one, I can't imagine a world big enough to hold such a library of books" (John 21:25). A life filled with doing good things has a ripple effect that keeps on going.

Life gets complicated. And in the complexity of our lives, we can forget the sheer power of deciding to live in the life-giving way: to do good, to serve others, and to love well.

Maybe we've added too much to Jesus. Take heart to this fact: The simple good that Jesus did with His one life brought genuine transformation and life recovery to millions of people. If we think in extreme or even complicated terms about our life purpose, we may miss out on the very basic ways we can seek to experience the life Jesus lived.

We should do good because Jesus did good. We serve others in the same way that we have been served. We can love others because we now know what real love is—that God loved us first. Jesus showed us what real love is and how real love acts. It's really not that complicated at all. By choosing to do good, serve others, and love people well, we are not only following Jesus "in His steps," but we are also continuing the mission He started, which the world needs today.

CAN WE LIVE THIS WAY TODAY?

But what does it mean to do good in a time filled with terrorist attacks, a complex global economy, and busy everyday life? What does doing good look like in a culture obsessed with self-promotion and self-advancement?

To do good is to choose the ethics of Jesus over the ways of the world. Exploiting migrant workers for the good of the company—is that good? Wall Street executives hoarding and amassing personal fortunes worth more than small nations—is that good? Health care for the wealthy but no care for the poor—is that good? Good is not based on politics or a political party. Good is found in the ways we see Jesus moving in His own life and in ours and upon the teachings He offered. His is an upside-down kingdom that preaches forgiveness when wronged, turning the cheek when angered, and living by your word, not by contracts.

Jim has lived with the guilt of feeling like he never really did enough with his life. He was never able to go on a mission trip overseas or to serve his church as an elder or deacon because of his long work hours. Though the desire to do good was in his heart, Jim confided to me that he always felt he came up short of having an impact and living with a life purpose greater than simply making a living. Jim and I met for several sessions and discussed his yearning to be able to do more with his life. At one session a few months ago, I introduced Jim to Luke's short synopsis of the life of Jesus: "[Jesus] went around doing good." I asked Jim how he'd feel if he could adopt this life purpose statement as his own. He agreed to give this new life purpose a trial run.

Jim has now shared with me the results of this thirty-day experiment, as we called it. "Steve, I look at people a whole new way now. Instead of seeing that my assistant's job is to do good stuff for me, I've reversed it. Now, each day, I ask how can I do good for her. I've changed the way I look at my colleagues in the same way. I start each day with this thought: *Today I choose to do good to the people who cross my path.*

Every Thursday evening my friend Lee seeks to do some good. He visits a good friend in his church who was diagnosed with ALS, more commonly known as Lou Gehrig's disease. It's an agonizing and slow death for those who have this disease. The body loses control while the mind is still active. Lee goes to his friend's home, gives him a back rub, reads a few verses from the Bible, and prays with his friend for peace and comfort. It's not a mission trip. It's not feeding the poor. It's a simple act of love—like a cup of cold water to a friend who is dying for the thirst of love. Lee gives the cup, and it costs him sixty minutes a week. That's it.

It's not hard to imagine a revolution beginning if followers of Jesus would simply choose to do good each day. Our perspectives would change, and our new way of living would bring life back to us.

Christie is mother to three children under five years of age. She's now trying to do good, serve others, and love well as a mom who has chosen to put her career on hold until her children are older. With her children, she bakes some cupcakes each week and delivers them to any new neighbors who move in to her community and to some older people in her church who no longer drive. "The older people really enjoy seeing my kids and greeting them as we deliver the cupcakes," she told me.

But you don't have to make cupcakes to do good. I don't bake and don't want to learn how to bake. For me, doing good requires me to change how I look at people I pass by, to treat people with more respect, and to choose to be kind in situations such as driving a car in heavy traffic or standing in a long line at the grocery store. Further, this requires me to really choose each day to treat my coworkers with dignity, honor, and service in helping them fulfill their own tasks and goals as well as managing my own work in the office. Doing good also means rethinking my status as a neighbor in my neighborhood. Rather than shutting my garage door and closing out the rest of the world when I arrive home, can I do something good for my elder neighbor who is unable to do the things he could do a few years ago? Can I help him roll his garbage out to the street? Can I help my other neighbors when something goes wrong in their lives? Can I say "Thank you," "Please may I …," and "How can I help you?" Can I choose to simply be nice? If we find it too hard to be nice and to do good to people, then we are taking ourselves far too seriously!

To do good is to see everything turned upside down in the world's economy. It can even seem baffling and arresting to witness someone doing good for the simple sake of doing good. This way of living reminds me of the Puritan prayer "The Valley of Vision":

> Let me learn by paradox that the way down is the
> way up, that to be low is to be high, that the broken
> heart is the healed heart, that the contrite spirit is the
> rejoicing spirit, that the repenting soul is the victori-
> ous soul, that to have nothing is to possess all, that to
> bear the cross is to wear the crown, that to give is to
> receive, that the valley is the place of vision.

If I am truly to do good, then I must choose not to gossip or bring to the light what God would want covered by grace. I cannot judge my brother for not following the way I think is right because it may, in fact, be wrong. People who demand that their way is the only right way perhaps stand the most to lose, because what if God's way is not your way or my way?

Retired bishop Rueben P. Job wrote,

> To abandon the way of the world and follow the way of Jesus is a bold move and requires honest, careful, and prayerful consideration.… Jesus himself told us to consider carefully the cost of discipleship: "For which of you, intending to build a tower, does not first sit down and estimate the cost, to see whether he has enough to complete it? … So therefore, none of you can become my disciple if you do not give up all your possessions" (Luke 14:28, 33).[50]

To choose to simply do good is a bold move on our part because it requires giving up the expectation that we will be rightfully rewarded. Giving up the possession of our expectations shaped by culture, nationality, and the darkness of our own hearts is fundamental to living the Jesus life.

Doing good does not require that we attempt to model the life of Mother Teresa, Saint Francis of Assisi, or another noble person. It begins for each of us as a daily choice: I will do good to the people I encounter today. That is the Jesus way. Paul supported this way of life: "For we are God's handiwork, created in Christ Jesus *to do good works*, which God prepared in advance for us to do" (Eph. 2:10 NIV). That is the way to live—to involve ourselves in simple acts of going good. We know in our hearts that we have done the right thing. Our consciences are at peace. Our hearts are emboldened, and our minds do not condemn us. By doing good, we choose to live well.

SERVE OTHERS

Sometimes people will recognize us for the good we have done. But the true test is when we do good in anonymity without the hope of acknowledgment. That too is the Jesus way.

Doing good is not primarily about acts of service, whether recognized or not, but about reposturing the heart. It begins with attitude, not action. If action compels us to do good, then we may do good for wrong reasons. We might want recognition. We might want our names on a plaque or printed in a bulletin. The heart is deceptive, and even the motivation for doing good things should be exposed to the penetrating light of Jesus.

To do good is to have the heart posture that everyone we encounter is an image bearer of God and thus should be treated like one. Think of a world where every day millions of people make a vow to do good. Instead of waving our fists in anger at the person who cuts us off on the drive to work, we will do good to them—and to our blood pressure! Instead of demeaning those around us who have seemingly less important jobs, we will do good to the janitor, the assistant, the temporary worker in the office.

I'm thinking of my dear friend Jim as I write this. Jim has been a follower of Jesus for years. He serves his church by helping people in the inner city. He rakes leaves for a widow who lives downtown. He mentors a young engaged couple. He does good things. Yet in my private conversations with him, he never feels like he is doing "enough." He compares his life to the lives of speakers who come to his church and share their stories about going to Africa to help HIV victims or to Haiti to help in the earthquake relief. He can never quite feel that his raking leaves for the widow compares in any way with missionaries who seem to have "given their all." I know Jim's heart well. He's been my friend for over ten years now and the good he has done for me shouts loud and clear in my heart. Jim is living the Jesus life every time he chooses to do good and serve someone, even in nonspectacular and unapplauded ways.

◆

To chose to walk in the way of serving by doing good requires a complicated fight against our nature that demands others to do good unto us. This inner battle is seen in the very temptation Jesus faced when He was alone in the desert and Satan showed Him an easier way to live than the way He was about to embark on. Satan's temptations were about comfort, position, and power—the same temptations that every follower of Christ faces when he or she chooses to live in the Jesus way.

Ideally when I decide to do good to you, my fear of being left out, forgotten, or ignored is not what motivates me. I'm doing good not in the hope that you'll reciprocate but because I choose to serve you. I choose to do good through serving because it is the Jesus way, not because I hope for reward.

However, fear coated with selfishness and egocentrism seizes our initiative and tries to persuade us that no one will do good to us. Consequently we tell ourselves there is no point to serving someone else. We reverse the ideal and lower the standard. Then we take the position that when someone does good to us, we'll repay the person with the favor of an act of kindness. That is not the right motivation for doing good.

I often hear people say, "I hope to hear the words spoken to me by God when I arrive in heaven, 'Well done, good and faithful servant.'" But even that is not pure motivation to do good. We know that heaven is not granted us because of what we do, no matter how good or righteous our deeds are (Titus 3:5). If we are seeking validation from God for our good works, we have a hidden agenda that benefits ourselves. The human heart gets so twisted that we follow another way we think will lead us to life, rather than following Jesus. Choosing to simply do good as Jesus did is to renounce the temptation that says, "Life is about me."

To choose to serve and do good is to choose to be in the way that leads to life, not death. We don't do good or serve so that we can have the feeling of satisfaction that we have done a good thing. We serve because people need to be served, people need to be loved, people need for their feet to be washed. Our service identifies us as a different people group than those who demand to be served first. As the people of God, our motivation is to be like Jesus and to follow in His steps. To serve and do good leads to a fulfillment we know only as we take on the posture of living the Jesus life.

Philo of Alexandria is credited with saying, "Be kind, for everyone you meet is fighting a great battle." The great battles Jesus faced in the lives of the men and women He encountered called for kindness, not brutality; goodness, not selfishness; and investment, not neglect. Today we encounter the battles for the hearts of men and women and children. The battles of depression, bankruptcy, stress, emotional wounds from the past, the challenges to make ends meet, health crises, relational failures, and others claim many, many prisoners of these great wars. Our acts of kindness and goodness are the right way. They are the manifestations of the continued incarnation of Jesus through us—through our hands—to a world in need. In so doing, touching, and giving, we find ourselves more alive.

LOVE WELL

We do not do good because we seek rewards.

We do not do good because we get something out of it for ourselves.

We do not do good even because we seek God's approval.

What, then, is our truest motivation? We do good because we follow Jesus and we seek to live the Jesus life.

Following Jesus is not *just* about believing the right things. Following Jesus is about being loved and extending love.

To do good is to keep in mind and heart the second greatest commandment that Jesus offered us in defining how a lover of God should live: "Love others as well as you love yourself" (Mark 12:31). That is the task of what it means to do good.

Love is the most powerful force in the world. It will cause a man to drop to his knees, smitten by the love for and with a woman and to spend the rest of their lives together in marriage. We do not *make* love. Love has its beginnings in God and is made there in the midst of the Trinity, where Father, Son, and Spirit exist in a perfect, harmonious, life-giving relationship with each other. Our desire to be united and to experience the union of ourselves—physically and emotionally—with one another has its genesis in the Trinity. We want to belong. We desire to be accepted. We long to be valued. We yearn to experience love.

While the Trinity experiences perfect love, we, not being as holy as God, experience a love that is less than His. We mess up. We hurt each other. We say things that wound and do things that offend. The gnawing need of human beings is to experience perfect love—the love of God in which we are accepted, celebrated, wanted, and valued. Perfect love happens only in relationship with God. As much as we think another person can fill God's shoes and love us in all the ways we need to be loved, only God can love us this way.

◆

Craig is a forty-five-year-old pastor. He has spent his life trying to convince others that God loves them. Yet somehow Craig never grasped for himself the fact that God loved him. As I heard Craig's story, it became obvious that his heart was barren of this message. Over the course of our time together, Craig awakened to this transformational truth. He told me, "Steve, I always thought God was disappointed in me and always wanted me to do more for Him, *then* maybe I could sense His love." Craig's experience is not unique. Many people live with feelings of God being disappointed in them rather than the acceptance of His love. When we accept God's love then offer it to others, we are participating in the divine love story—that God loves us passionately and longs to express His love to us.

Jesus offered this way and in turn invited us to extend this kind of love to others: "This is my command: Love one another the way I loved you" (John 15:12). In saying this, Jesus told us to walk in the way of love throughout all of our lives and to give this love to others. When we do this, it is proof that we are in the Jesus way.

Years later, the aging apostle John wrote,

> My beloved friends, let us continue to love each other since love comes from God. Everyone who loves is born of God and experiences a relationship with God. The person who refuses to love doesn't know the first thing about God, because God is love—so you can't know him if you don't love. This is how God showed his love for us: God sent his only Son into the world so we might live through him. This is the kind of love we are talking about—not that we once upon a time loved God, but that he loved us and sent his Son as a sacrifice to clear away our sins and the damage they've done to our relationship with God. (1 John 4:7–10)

We are invited into the way of love, and love is our mark of validation. The greatest demonstration of love is seen in how John described it: God showed His love in sending us Jesus. There would be no gospel, no good news, were it not for God giving us His only Son in love—"This is how much God loved the world: He gave his Son, his one and only Son" (John 3:16).

God acted with goodness toward us not because He needed approval or would get anything for Himself out of it. He acted with goodness to serve us. He gave for our sakes. Love motivated God to do what He did. He loved us well.

I've often heard people express their initial experience of God's love this way: "I accepted Jesus Christ to be my Savior and Lord." But perhaps the real truth is this: "I experienced the love of God through encountering Jesus Christ."

I use the words *experience* and *encounter* because true love is more than a mere mental assent to saying that you believe something is true. True love is much deeper, and it moves us. When Matthew, Peter, James, and John first encountered the love of Jesus in their ordinary lives while doing their ordinary activities, that love made everything different from that time forward.

Only love transforms. Information cannot transform a person. No matter how many seminars you attend, books you read, and notebooks you fill up over the course of your life, sheer information will not change you. Jesus knew this. He loved. And transformation of ordinary lives into extraordinary lives was the result. Life is morphed into the richest descriptive words Jesus could use when He said, "I have come that they may have life, and have it to the full" (John 10:10 NIV).

The way of love is the way of experiencing a full life—not an ordinary life. Life without love is not really life, because God never intended for anyone of those whom He loved to go through life without experiencing or offering love to others. The way to really live is to really love.

This kind of *agape* love, however, must be taught as well as caught. Because humans have not encountered this kind of love and have offered only a lower form of love as brotherly (*phila*) or sexual (*eros*), we have to relearn how love looks, acts, and feels. Some of us have been shaped in unhealthy love that is codependent and conditional. That is precisely why in God's great love He allowed for us to be transformed by the renewing of our minds (Rom. 12:2). We can relearn and experience this great love then offer it to others. When we see great love lived out in front of our eyes, it catches our attention. It's more than learning or memorizing a new definition. Love is deeper and captures both the mind and the heart.

Jesus' followers who lived in Corinth must have had a great deficiency in what real love looked like. They confused love to the extent that they had adopted and incorporated some of the cultural ways to love that were clearly not love at all. So Paul spelled it out for them in black and white. He put the cookies on the lowest shelf possible and broke down God's love:

> Love never gives up.
> Love cares more for others than for self.
> Love doesn't want what it doesn't have.
> Love doesn't strut,
> Doesn't have a swelled head,
> Doesn't force itself on others,
> Isn't always "me first,"
> Doesn't fly off the handle,
> Doesn't keep score of the sins of others,
> Doesn't revel when others grovel,
> Takes pleasure in the flowering of truth,
> Puts up with anything,
> Trusts God always,

Always looks for the best,

Never looks back,

But keeps going to the end. (1 Cor. 13:4–7)

By rethinking and reenvisioning your life, perhaps now it is possible to truly do good, serve others, and love people well. In doing so, you will be participating in the ongoing life of Jesus today—Jesus' life being lived out through your own!

LIVING THE JESUS LIFE RIGHT NOW

1. Consider doing the thirty-day experiment. For the next thirty days, gather a few of your friends, and each day choose to do good, serve others, and love well. See how this experiment affects your life and the lives of those around you. Share with each other your progress, and try to journal your experience so you can reflect upon any changes you witness in your life. Can you extend the time frame for a longer experiment and monitor what happens in and around you?

2. To remind you of the simple choice to *do good*, *serve others*, and *love well*, write these three phrases down on a small index card or piece of paper. Place it in a visible place such as your bathroom mirror, refrigerator door, or automobile dashboard.

3. Do a survey of your life by asking yourself the following questions:

    a. Who in my life needs good things done for them?

    b. How can I do good for my neighbors and friends?

    c. What do I need to start doing in order to do good, serve others, and love well?

    d. What do I need to stop doing in order to do good, serve others, and love well?

4. Ask your closest friends to comment on how you interact with them. You may want to ask them, "How do you see me doing good? How do you see me serving you and others? How do you experience me loving well?" Ask for honest feedback and their ideas on how you can improve.

THE WAY OF RITUAL

Creating Signposts as We Journey through Life

*He went to Nazareth, where he had been brought up, and on the
Sabbath day he went into the synagogue, **as was his custom**.*

—Luke 4:16 (NIV)

We tend to forget, if not ignore, the Jewishness of Jesus. In our
efforts to make everything relevant, we have forgotten that being a
follower of Jesus is not a new fad or even new way of having faith.
It's anchored in a rich history, one filled with practices, habits, and
customs that we know little about today.

Author Philip Yancey wrote,

> I can no more understand Jesus apart from his
> Jewishness than I can understand Gandhi apart from
> his Indianness. I need to go back, way back, and pic-
> ture Jesus as a first-century Jew with a phylactery on
> his wrist and Palestinian dust on his sandals.[51]

We need to reenvision Jesus so that we can jettison our illusions of Him as a white middle-class American. Jesus was not an
American. His Jewishness permeated everything He said, did, and
lived. And embedded in this way of life, we find signposts and clues
to help us rediscover our way to the life we are searching for.

You can relax. I am not going to give you a crash course in historical Judaism. You can read that elsewhere.[52] But I am going to explore the rich meaning of rituals and their role in our living faith and our need for them.

A ritual is "the performance of ceremonial acts prescribed by tradition or by sacerdotal decree. Ritual is a specific, observable mode of behaviour."[53] Rituals are familiar and recognized acts, events, and traditions that help us have meaning, tie us together, and interpret through symbols what is happening in and around us. They are as simple as the lighting of birthday candles and as complex as the ceremonies surrounding the burial of presidents and royalty. In our fast-paced and busy lives, the neglect of certain life-giving and life-interpreting rituals causes us to skim the surface of our lives rather than establish deep roots that can anchor and hold us—especially during life's storms.

We should never forget or ignore that the Christian faith was rooted securely in Judaism. The early church took on the same form as the ancient Jewish synagogue. Praying the hours, or the daily office, is anchored in the Jewish hours of prayers. Jesus prayed the Psalms and knew the writings of the prophets. He was well versed in the Old Testament and frequently used the Jewish writings as foundational planks for His revolutionary teachings and interpretations. Jesus never destroyed His Jewish roots but honored them, allowing a new, vibrant faith to be birthed directly from His heritage.

JESUS EXTENDS THE WAY TO LIFE THROUGH RITUALS

As we read the four biographies of Jesus and see the early actions of the New Testament church, we find rituals observed not out of mundane habit but as life-giving reminders of a bigger story. Life-giving rituals brought meaning, "Aha" moments of understanding, and invited the followers of Jesus to participate in something significant that was happening both in them and around them.

While Jesus was sinless and certainly did not need to be baptized as an outward symbol of His repentance, we see Him willingly participating in His own baptism by His cousin John. Following His baptism, the bud of Jesus' life and ministry bloomed. From that moment on, His vocational calling became public and His ministry truly began. For many, the ritual of baptism becomes a defining moment. Every time we witness a baptism, we can be reminded of our own. We remember that we too are the beloved of God. In a world filled with the message of "never enough" and filled with the voices of self-rejection and shame, baptism becomes a reminder of our true identity. One pastor I know encourages his members to remember their baptism when they wash their faces at night or in the morning each day.

We see Jesus using the ritual of prayer in both public and private. When He fed the multitudes, He gave thanks for the multiplied loaves and fish. We see Him often withdrawing for His own times of silence and solitude. We see Him laying hands on people who are sick and having meals with friends. Read the Gospels again for yourself and you may be surprised at how many rituals you can see Jesus using to help interpret reality for those around Him. He used the ritual of a wedding to teach us about God's provision and blessing in new wine. He used the ritual of a funeral to proclaim, "I am the resurrection and the life."

One of the most daring times that Jesus translated the ordinary into transformational truth is found in John 7. This feast was the one of the seven annual festivals that Jesus participated in for over thirty years. Every Jew was required to attend this event in Jerusalem, and the city itself swelled to overcapacity. "On the final and climactic day of the Feast," the high priest would ascend the steps in the temple in ceremonial fashion, taking a golden pitcher of water with him. At the prescribed time, the priest would pour out the water, watching it cascade and spiral down to the ground below him and in front of the thousands of people who gathered to watch.

In this setting, Jesus did the unthinkable. He stood and said in a loud voice, "If anyone thirsts, let him come to me and drink" (John 7:37). Jesus seized that precise moment and announced a transforming truth that changed everything in that particular ceremony and on until this very day. Jesus assumed a position of authority and "cried out" in a voice that shattered the collective silence and infused the ritual with new meaning. He spoke of new and living water not poured from a golden pitcher used only once a year. This new water would be continually available for them to drink through God's Spirit, who would reside in them soon. Jesus took the expected ritual yet defined it with a new and deeper meaning that no one expected.

How does Jesus do that? How did He seize a moment in time and create new meaning? He used a ritual to speak a new truth that gave us important and life-changing information. Jesus' water being offered was now far, far better. John tells us later that even the temple guards reported, "We've never heard anyone speak like this man" (John 7:46). Jesus took *a* moment, spoke into *the* moment—using the ordinary symbol of water—and everyone heard the true message He intended.

Throughout His ministry, Jesus transformed our understanding of ordinary, linear events in life and helped us experience the unfolding of the kingdom all around us—even within us.

On the last night of His earthly life, Jesus gathered His disciples at another time of ritual: Passover. He had made sure all the details about the meal were set. Jesus did little on the fly, I think, but especially not on this solemn night. He wanted to mark this special time like no other the disciples had experienced. For sure, they—even we—would never forget what was going to happen. They ate the expected and annual Passover meal in the traditional way. But suddenly Jesus took the bread and poured the cup of wine and filled them with a deeper, life-giving meaning. Once again He broke with what was customarily said and spoke something new, something life changing for those gathered. It was a communion like no one had ever experienced. That night, Jesus started a practice that continues to this day in our participation with the bread and cup. He commanded His followers to remember Him in the way He scripted this new understanding about the bread and the cup.

No matter what you call it, Communion, the Lord's Supper, or the Eucharist, the time of the bread and wine stops us in our tracks and we realize that we are actually participating in something Jesus told us to do. Jesus specifically asked us to *do* this in remembrance of Him. As we take Communion and share the Lord's Supper or feast upon the Eucharist, we are somehow transported to a place where we are in communion with the living Savior—another God-with-us moment that we so need in life.

There are many Jesus rituals we need to rediscover along the way in order to live the Jesus life. All of this should motivate us to want to read more about our Savior's life, know His ways, and find out how our own lives can have richer meaning. Just by participating in the way He did His life, our lives today take on much-needed sacredness and significance.

But today we've thrown the baby out with the bathwater and abandoned the richness of Jewish ways for our own. It is one clear reason that I believe we have become so lost in our ways, and it reveals our dire need to return to some roots where we can experience the life, joy, traditions, and rituals we have forsaken.

ONE ATTEMPT TO ESTABLISH A NEW RITUAL

When each of my four sons turned thirteen, my wife and I threw a festive dinner to commemorate this passage into manhood. We invited our friends, not theirs, to come to our home, and Gwen prepared that particular son's favorite foods. Each of our invited guests knew ahead of time to look for a symbolic gift to present to my son at the dinner. That night was all about the passage into manhood for our sons. One friend gave a compass. Another gave a flashlight. Some gave a special book that held meaning for them. After dinner we'd gather in our living room and place the son in the middle where each person would be able to bless him with words of affirmation, meaning, and validation. When we did this for our oldest son, the three others simply watched—probably in disbelief at the "cool stuff" and attention he received. But what really happened was much deeper. That night became a time the younger sons and the guests anticipated in their own lives. That night was monumental. A boy was recognized and ushered into manhood.

I'll never forget our youngest son, Leighton, telling Cameron, our third son, on his thirteenth birthday celebration, "Cam, I want to become a man like you are now." As Leighton said this to his brother, I knew in my heart that this rite of passage had taken root. Since then many of our friends have done something similar for their children.

The second and perhaps even more important part of the meaning of life celebration was taking each son, the week after this celebration, on a "meaning of life" trip. My gift to the celebrated son was the plane tickets, the brochures, and the itinerary for our trip together. During those years my interest was awakening to a great, wild West that I wanted to experience. I planned each trip so that I'd get to visit a different national park somewhere in the West. We'd camp each night and explore in the daytime. After dinner, we talked about what it means to be a man. Each night was a different topic: integrity, work, walking with God, sexual intimacy, and how to handle money. I'll never forget their eyes as I led them into the details and intricacies of being intimate with their future wives. On the night of the sex talk, we prayed for their wives-to-be.

Years later, I have no doubt that my sons will carry on this ritual with their own children. It seems etched in their hearts and epic in their minds. It's one of the most important things I think I've ever been able to do for my sons, something that hints at the word *legacy*.

RECLAIM LIFE THROUGH RITUAL

More and more, I see the importance of rituals to help us reclaim the life we are losing in our world today. Many of us just press on without really marking special occasions that foster life and nourish rich memories we can feed on throughout our lives. Without such festive times, we are simply left to the long, sometimes-exhausting journey of life. Rituals marked with celebration, significance, and sacredness fuel the fire within and enable us to do life well.

When the tyranny of the urgent usurps the important, we have taken the first steps off the path that leads to life and are moving toward a shallow, stagnant place. We lose our lives not in one dramatic sweep or one mistake but little by little by not doing the right things and making life-giving choices. It happens over a long period of time for most of us.

Our obsession with the culture of speed is dizzying, and we are losing our equilibrium. Life loses its meaning and we are reduced to a cynical view of life. Through osmosis we take in the values of the world around us rather than shape the world.

When life is difficult, as it often is, the meaning of life erodes and we lose our footing. We lose perspective on the larger story going on, and we assume a posture of survival—one foot in front of the next.

Our individualistic society shapes us to be lone rangers in life. We can become like the person described in the book of Revelation who has "a reputation for vigor and zest, but [is] dead" (Rev. 3:1). For most of us, this deadness does not happen overnight. We become dead when we stop doing the life-giving things that breathe the *ruach*—the breath of God—back into us.

The use of life-giving rituals is one of the ways we choose to live the abundant life each day. Rituals convey a message to the heart as well as to the mind. A ritual brings together the mundane with the powerful, the earthly with the spiritual. We use rituals to mark space and time. Rituals help us piece things together in life. When we practice rituals, we are connecting more than dots; we are connecting the past to the present and the present to the unknown future.

Rituals give meaning to moments. They remind us that what is happening is not ordinary but significant and that we need to wake up and pay attention to what is happening around us.

OUR NEED FOR LIFE-GIVING RITUALS

For some, the word *ritual* may stir up negative emotions and images. Perhaps you were shaped in a setting that went overboard with rituals that had little meaning. Some family rituals might have been fun and life-giving, while others were invitations to shame or compliance. It's important to understand the difference.

I remember a healthy ritual my dad practiced in his attempts to help our family do something together. He invited all of us to go on a Sunday-afternoon drive through the country. We'd all climb into his silver Buick station wagon and off we'd go. The highlight was stopping by the service station to gas up the car. However, the real reason for the stop was to go into the store and pick out a soft drink and candy bar. The drink and candy became a sort of communal experience that bonded us together—something we enjoyed and looked forward to each week. The car became an inescapable place where we were all together, enjoying our Cheerwine cherry-flavored cola drinks and PayDay candy bars as if we were at the altar in some cathedral.

Our lives are more than facts and linear events to memorize or recount. Healthy and life-giving rituals help us savor life, not just endure it. They help increase the quality of the time we have to live. Through them we gain the meaning, see the purpose, understand the season we are in, and learn to be thankful for what God brings each day—in each day. Life-giving rituals build bridges between the past and present, between individuals who are alone and those experiencing authentic fellowship together, and between varied and different people groups to become nations who live in solidarity.

As Eugene Peterson said, "We live in narrative, we live in story. Existence has a story shape to it. We have a beginning and an end, we have a plot, we have characters." Our faith is a story. The events of 9/11, earthquakes in Haiti, and economic downturns bring us to our knees. There is the tragedy of divorce and death, the celebration of birth and new beginnings, the scenes of failure and shame and also of transformation and hope. Rituals help us mark these events and move through to the healing we need.

As I write this, a mass killing has just happened in a Tuscon, Arizona, grocery store. The man who fired the bullets killed and maimed several people, altering lives in an instant. In the aftermath, the president flew to Tucson, where thousands had gathered and lit candles. Songs were sung and flags were dropped to half-mast. The president's speech was featured on every major media network. We were brought together as a country to grieve, recognize the solemnity of what had just happened, and recover our lost equilibrium. News commentators said the memorial service filled with the ritual of song and the president's attendance was "healing."

In my practice of seeing people for spiritual guidance and direction, I make it a custom to participate in a ritual in our beginning moments. I light a small candle to mark this time as different. I strike the match and bring it to the wick of the candle and say something like, "We need the Light of the World today to dispel our darkness. Come, Lord Jesus, be among us." One man, so enthusiastic about having our time together, grabbed the matches and lit the candle after I had stepped out of my office for a minute. The little ritual I had begun with him had taken root in his heart. He said, "Steve, I need this light so badly this week. I simply could not wait for the light to come." That simple act helped me sense his thirst and hunger. I will never forget his marking our time as a sacred conversation.

One megachurch created a ritual that has a great impact on thousands of people every time a funeral takes place. The church congregation includes many wealthy businesspeople but also has a growing number of poor men and women. As time passed, people took note of the fact that when a wealthy business leader died, flowers generously adorned the church's platform area. But when a poor, homeless woman died, there were no flowers—not even a few to make a spray for her casket. The leaders of the church now use a simple draping cloth for every casket. No flowers are allowed inside the sanctuary during a funeral. The casket pall, made of simple material with an embroidered cross, is a symbolic gesture many appreciate. The new ritual recognizes that in death, all people are equal. We all come into this world with nothing, and we all leave this world with nothing.

This is what rituals do—they communicate an unspoken truth to us that we need to hear with our hearts.

EXPLORING LIFE-GIVING RITUALS

Rituals do not come in a one-size-fits-all format. The people who use the rituals need to define them. They can be individualized and custom-made to fit a person, group, family, church, denomination, or organization.

The place to begin is simply to look for rituals you're already doing and practicing. What are you already doing that meets the criteria I have described? How do you celebrate birthdays, important events, and tenure of service? How does your family meet together for meals and prepare to enjoy the mealtime together? How do you put your children to bed at night? If you're single, what do you already do to build community into your life or acknowledge the meaning of your experiences?

Just as the Jews, including Jesus' family, lit a candle to symbolize the Sabbath's arrival, my wife and I have tried to do the same. We light our "Sabbath candle" every time we practice our Sabbath time. The Sabbath candle becomes a visual reminder for us that this day is set aside for us to cease from the regular work activities of the week. It preaches the one-word sentence: "Cease!" Cease what you're doing and begin to live differently on this much-needed day. The candle shines, reminding us that this day is going to be different. We need it to be different!

It's important to own the life stage and season you're currently in. If you have small children and are in a dual-career marriage, be gentle with yourself and simply begin to find ways to incorporate life-giving times. If you are in the empty-nest stage of life where many of your old life-giving rituals are now simply not possible, what new ones can you build into your life that will honor your current life as well as treasure the life you have already lived?

Gwen and I are in this stage. Our last son just moved out of our home. With no kids around, my temptation was, "Let's just get our dinner and go watch the news." In doing this, we surrendered the time that for thirty years had been a sacred ritual of being together. The TV became the third partner in our marriage. We discovered that we talked less, we felt disconnected from each other, and a distance widened between us. The main reason was because we had abandoned our ritual of simply gathering around the table and talking. So we went back to gathering once more at our table for six, just the two of us sitting together. We still light our candle and now talk again about our day, share our dreams and desires, and often pray for our children and their new marriages and challenges. Simply put, to give up our ritual of a mealtime together is to give up more than the food we share.

BUILDING RITUALS THAT BREATHE LIFE

To discover and practice rituals that breathe life and not drain life, think through these building blocks:

Building Block 1: Purpose. What is the purpose of commemorating the event? Do you want to celebrate a friend's or family member's birthday or anniversary? What symbolizes this past event you lived through? Perhaps your friend was fired or got a promotion. Is there a symbol you can incorporate into the time shared together? When I was fired from what I thought was my dream job, my wife and I opened up the last link of a chain, symbolizing that I was now free to do what I really wanted to do. We later started using the chain as a Christmas-tree ornament, and when I hang it, I always remember the paradox of fear and courage I felt when the wall came tumbling down and thought it would bury me. Thankfully it didn't.

Building Block 2: Frequency. How frequently will you observe the occasion? Gwen and I light a candle in the morning hours of our Sabbath. The candle has become both a conversation piece and a light to mark a special day of ceasing for us. Birthdays and anniversaries are annual events, but what other events could you recognize monthly, quarterly, or annually? What about a day for your family to be together—but without friends or neighbors? How often would you want to do this?

As I mentioned in chapter 2, I get to see one of my closest friends only once a year because we live two thousand miles apart. But we've decided that our friend time will be like one of the Jewish feasts. We eat together, enjoy time together, pray together, and share the story of our year in person and not through email.

Building Block 3: Touch. What sensory element would enhance the ritual's meaning? Do you need music, a candle, a certain meaningful jacket? Should you arrange the furniture in a different way? How about the lighting?

On a retreat with some friends, I was presented with a special, comfortable blue denim shirt. My friends simply said, "Steve, we want you to wear this when you speak and travel to remind you that you are not alone; we are your brothers who are praying with you and standing with you. As you wear this shirt, remember who you are." They had obviously thought about this long before we gathered together.

Each year at Christmas, one of our family's rituals was to present each of our sons with a special ornament that somehow symbolized his year the way we saw it. Now each son has a box of ornaments, and as each son marries, we present the box to his wife for them to start their own traditions and rituals together. While the ornaments are not expensive, each one symbolizes a life well lived that year—a year of our child's life so far.

Building Block 4: Words. Find the words to connect to the symbol. Not all of us are good at being extemporaneous. Most of us need time to communicate well. The right words spoken at the right time are like "apples of gold in settings of silver" (Prov. 25:11 NIV). Words converged with symbols help transform ordinary time into sacred time. It's amazing to see how often this is practiced throughout the Bible. Moses was a master in knowing how to tell people what manna really was. David was an artist in taking a simple bleating sheep and helping us identify with our need for a Shepherd. Jeremiah used the clay of the earth to help us grasp the shaping of our lives. Ezekiel used the "dry bones" to help us connect with our own desperate need to live.

My sister Gloria was a schoolteacher for over thirty years in a large North Carolina city. She spent her entire working life in a small green trailer teaching boys and girls how to read, write, and do math. Her ritual for each day was to place her hand on the doorknob of her schoolroom trailer before she would begin her day and simply recite, "God, go before me in this room and be present before I enter." She had purpose, frequency, touch, and words, and the ritual sustained her in her work. Twice she was recognized as teacher of the year in her district.

Developing and participating in life-giving rituals takes some courage. Trust me, for me to light a candle in my office in front of a medical doctor, insurance salesperson, or plumber still makes me wince nearly every time I do it. But I am reminded in those moments to take heart and simply move forward. As we, like Jesus, take courage to give meaning to our friends and family around us, new life bubbles up. We put words to actions and connect dots long before we're disconnected. We blur the lines of the ordinary with the sacred, and we feel life welling up within us. Our own personal meaning converges with spiritual truth, and we want to kneel because something holy has happened, something good. We see life as it really is.

THE WAY OF SUFFERING
Understanding the Role of Pain and Suffering

To this you were called, because Christ suffered for you, leaving
you an example, that you should follow in his steps.

—1 Peter 2:21 (NIV)

JESUS AND THE WAY OF SUFFERING

Despised. Rejected. A man of suffering. Familiar with pain.

These are the words Isaiah chose to describe God's Chosen One, the Savior of the world (Isa. 53:3 NIV). It seems unthinkable that Jesus would be subjected to a life of suffering and scorn. And it's often unacceptable to think of suffering as one of the ways we have to embrace in order to truly live. It's been said that suffering presents the greatest obstacle and challenge to a living faith in God. We'd prefer escape. We think a good life is a life immune from suffering. What's striking is to realize that the very life of Jesus began in sorrow and suffering.

If you watch news on TV, you've noticed that graphic artists brush out the faces of children who are crime victims. We're careful not to be too graphic, too insensitive to the viewers. Yet Jewish mothers and fathers did not have this feature to erase Herod's atrocities when Jesus was born. Read the story of the slaughter of the innocents in Matthew 2:13–18. No church Christmas pageant contains this horrible scene. We prefer little lambs, chubby angels, and a nice, neat stall with regal wise men dressed in colorful royal robes. Not blood, guts, and decapitated babies tossed about. But Matthew's gospel reveals the truth. Jesus was born into a time of unparalleled agony when brutal and insecure King Herod ordered the murder of all male children two years old or younger.

Take a look at Peter Paul Rubens's famous painting titled "The Massacre of the Innocents,"[54] and you'll find muscular Roman soldiers grabbing helpless babies from their frightened mothers and violently throwing them to the ground. You'll see limbs and heads littered like unwanted trash. One soldier in the center of the painting has his drawn sword on the neck of an innocent victim. This fear fueled the hearts of Joseph and Mary to protect Jesus by fleeing to Egypt, away from friends and family, to live as displaced parents of the very Son of God. These were the beginning days of Jesus—born into a troubled time and shaped early by displacement.

FAMILIAR WITH PAIN

We're glad to read the account of Jesus opening His ministry by unrolling the scrolls of Isaiah and reading the words:

> The Spirit of the Lord is on me, because he has anointed me to proclaim good news to the poor. He has sent me to proclaim freedom for the prisoners and recovery of sight for the blind, to set the oppressed free, to proclaim the year of the Lord's favor. (Luke 4:18–19 NIV)

But we forget that immediately after Jesus did this, "all the people in the synagogue were furious.... They got up, drove him out of the town, and took him to the brow of the hill on which the town was built, in order to throw him off the cliff" (Luke 4:28–29 NIV).

Rejection was not just something Jesus experienced during His Passion Week. What we learn through a careful rereading of the Gospels is that suffering, rejection, being despised, and being forsaken were all present throughout Jesus' life. Sadly Jesus' very own siblings joined in this kind of activity, once even calling Him crazy while He was teaching (Mark 3:21). Pain dealt at the hand of the family in which we are born is perhaps the cruelest of all. There in the family, of all places, we'd hope to find acceptance, unconditional love, and grace. But Jesus found none of these.

These kinds of experiences lodged in Jesus' soul and heart and caused Him to lament about His conditions: "Foxes have dens and birds have nests, but the Son of Man has no place to lay his head" (Luke 9:58 NIV). This homeless man, who began this saga of rejection and suffering within months of His birth, would continue His suffering sojourn throughout His entire life. There was no safe place for Jesus, and as we see His life unfold, there were few safe people.

He chose twelve men to become His closest associates, yet one would betray Him, another would doubt Him, still another would repeatedly reject Him, and all would be slow to believe Him. Jesus would plead for His friends to stay awake with Him in His personal moment of spiraling despair and desperate prayers for God's intervention, but they would sleep, leaving Jesus alone and forsaken again (Luke 22:39–46).

One of the saddest scenes recorded for us is in Luke 22. It concerns the night when Jesus shared the Jewish Passover with His disciples. Jesus was diligent to prepare the details of this special feast. We enter an intimate dinner scene with Jesus and His closest associates reclining at the table. It was Passover. A time of remembering, reflecting, and feasting. Yet it was here when Jesus changed everything. He gave new and sobering meaning to the bread on the table, telling His friends that His body would be soon broken like the bread. His blood would be poured out like the wine in the cup. We can imagine the silence as new meaning began to dawn on the disciples. Bread is His body. Wine is His blood.

We'd think that sober mood would continue through the late night. But what happens is an argument and power struggle. In what should have been an intimate moment of true fellowship and sharing, "a dispute ... arose among them as to which of them was considered to be greatest" (Luke 22:24 NIV). What happened was not a toast to thank Jesus for all He had done. No worship service or time of testimonies to share all the good memories. It's heartbreaking that the closest companions to Jesus argued like schoolchildren—as men starved more for control than their own transformations. Jesus could not find solace or reprieve from His closest friends. Sometimes this might be true for us seeking to live the Jesus life. When people fail us, only God is our rock, our solace, our healer, our advocate, our true Savior.

Look at any crucifix and you'll be reminded of what happened next. More rejection. More physical torture. Nails and the cross. Agonizing thirst because Jesus was crucified in the heat of the day, and the sun lingered for hours until He finally died.

When I was fired from the position that seemed to be the end all–fix all role that I had dreamed about for years, my life crashed. I spiraled into a dark depression thinking my life was over. I went to my spiritual director for guidance. After I told him my story, he simply handed me a rugged crucifix and asked me to hold it. As a Baptist boy, I had never, ever held such a thing in my life until that moment. We sat quietly for what seemed like an eternity. As I stared at the crucifix with the tortured body of Jesus fixed upon it, something connected deep inside of me. Jesus knew suffering. Jesus knew my suffering. We were connected through suffering. My spiritual director simply said quietly, "Now you understand *His* rejection, don't you?" I remember precisely praying these words, "Jesus, You do know the feeling, don't You?"

I want to know if you belong—or feel abandoned.

—David Whyte, "Self-Portrait"

Over the course of our marriage, Gwen and I have buried her mother and my father. She's been diagnosed with breast cancer and I feared for her life and my aloneness. Three of our adult sons are army officers, having fought in the Iraq and Afghanistan wars. Without a doubt, parenting men-children who were fighting in a war was the hardest season of parenting we have experienced. We feared the black army cruiser pulling up into our driveway to tell us that one of our sons had been killed. We lived in this tension for years—not weeks. We had sleepless nights and agonizing days, knowing that they were out on a mission. We feared for their lives and found consolation in our times of prayer, silence, and reading the Bible.

As a pastor, I've held the hands of countless people who were in their last moments of earthly life. Some wanted to be left alone, and some wanted hymns sung. We've witnessed starvation in third-world countries and tsunamis in others. We've felt the sting and blow of suffering, and as we grow older, it is not getting any easier.

Two of my closest friends lost their battles with cancer while I have been writing this book. Both were Christian leaders and outstanding contributors to the message of Jesus Christ. Yet from my perspective, both died too young, and their absence has compounded my sadness. One was my friend Rick, who was forty-six years old and had a wife and two teenage daughters. The doctors tried everything to stop the cancer. Not so long ago Rick had assumed the helm of a major Christian ministry where he thought God was preparing him to serve for the rest of his life. But no one suspected the rest of his life would be so short. It hadn't occurred to Rick that he would never walk his daughters down the aisle when they marry or see his grandchildren when they are born. Rick and I wanted to grow old together as friends. He wanted more to his life than he obviously got. I went to visit him before he passed away. He was suffering and suffering badly. The pain meds were only taking the edge off. He was in constant pain that was agonizing and completely debilitating.

Just last week Gwen was told by a surgeon that she will have to undergo complex spine surgery to correct three different problems all converging at the same time. It was not the news we wanted or needed. Major and "complicated surgery" was the only alternative for her agonizing pain. Life was going to be interrupted. During that same week, my editor called and invited me for lunch. As we sat in my favorite restaurant, the mood turned sober: "Steve, the manuscript is not going to work." I had turned in the manuscript thinking I'd done a great job in the initial draft. But when my editor read it, he thought otherwise. As he talked, I saw my summer plans of going to Grand Teton National Park and seeing the moose, bear, and elk drink from Jenny Lake ebb into oblivion. My heart sank, and I felt depressed. The life I wanted to live was being robbed from me. I would have to "rewrite, redo, restructure the entire manuscript." All my plans sank in one lunch. Everything in my life changed in one single week.

It happens that way, doesn't it? One phone call, one email, one doctor's visit that changes everything. The good life we have worked so hard to enjoy is suddenly gone—right before our eyes.

I well remember Beverly weeping in my arms at her husband's sudden and unexpected death. She said through the tears, "I never, ever thought I'd be a widow so young." We seldom imagine how life can turn on a dime and change everything. But when it happens— and it will—we are tempted to believe the lie: "Your life is over. Life will never be the same. All your dreams are now destroyed." That lie eats away at the Jesus life. It erodes our belief and our confidence and robs us of joy. But what we learn in living the Jesus life is that suffering is not the end of the story. It wasn't for Jesus, and it will not be for us.

We learn in life that our security is not in the chronology of the years but in the attitude of our hearts. A good life is not amassed in living longer or perhaps "better" than your friends. A good life is not dependent upon counting all the places you've visited or even completing your "bucket list"—a list of all the things you want to do and see before you die.

A life that is blessed by God, empowered by the Spirit, and lived according to the ways of Jesus Christ is a life that accepts the fact that life is fragile. We are but dust, just as the Bible says, and any breath we have and take is not just a breath but also a gift given us by God.

STIRRING THE POT OF DEEP AND DARK QUESTIONS

To grow in the Jesus life is to grow *through* suffering, not around it. We grow through suffering and receive the lessons that only suffering can teach us no matter how hard we might try to avoid, ignore, or run from its grip. Suffering has a way of pressing our clay, pinching off our false assumptions, and smashing beliefs that are simply not true. When the Potter's wheel starts whirling and we sense suffering is just ahead, we can either scream to get off, which rarely happens in a good potter's studio, or allow the hands of suffering to do what only they can do—reshape our lives into better, albeit different, forms.

Let us be clear on this. Suffering by itself is not what makes a person a saint. As we learn to "walk in His steps," which will invariably lead to degrees of heartache, we learn to accept that there is a larger life we are living into as we take each step. This is not a life immune from suffering but one that is able to endure it because of what we have received through the suffering and on the other side of the suffering. This is precisely why Peter, Paul, and James all converged in a unified voice to tell us that we should not fear suffering but embrace it as a part of the Jesus life. Peter said that Christ's suffering leaves us an example. Paul wrote, "We also glory in our sufferings, because we know that suffering produces perseverance; perseverance, character; and character, hope. And hope does not put us to shame, because God's love has been poured out into our hearts through the

Holy Spirit, who has been given to us" (Rom. 5:3–5 NIV). And James recorded, "Consider it a sheer gift, friends, when tests and challenges come at you from all sides. You know that under pressure, your faith-life is forced into the open and shows its true colors. So don't try to get out of anything prematurely. Let it do its work so you become mature and well-developed, not deficient in any way" (James 1:2–4).

THE WORK THAT ONLY SUFFERING CAN DO

Rather than choosing to actually live the Jesus life, we can choose to live in certain illusions that are shaped more by culture and charismatic leaders than rooted in truth. Such illusions include:

- Christians should not have to suffer.
- When we seek to live in God's will, God will protect us from suffering.
- Suffering means that the one suffering has does something wrong and is being punished.
- There simply is no point or sense in someone having to unjustly suffer in this life.

When set alongside the Bible, these statements are proved false. The Bible gives witness to men and women who dealt with catastrophe, war, illness, premature death, and unjust suffering. One thing is for certain, if we are serious in our attempt to live the Jesus life, we need to figure out how suffering fits into the life we want to live.

Like Jacob, we may wrestle this question out with God until He blesses us with an answer that will satisfy us. But what we will learn is that this question may never be answered this side of eternity. We may, in fact, wrestle all of our lives with the questions about why people suffer. And the older we become, combined with the more suffering we see and perhaps personally experience, the question morphs from Why does suffering happen? to When will *I* suffer and how will *I* handle it?

We must reject easy answers to life's hardest questions. We must admit that such questions are hard to reconcile with the tensions we know. To live the Jesus life well means we will have to jettison easy answers and pious platitudes about suffering. We will accept the wrestling as an ongoing part of our very lives. In the wrestling comes an assurance of God's presence that says, "Even though we are in pain, God has not abandoned us. He is the God-With-Us, and that means even in and through hard times."

At first, this may seem risky, if not foolish. Who of us doesn't really love an easy answer to life's most pressing questions? But when it comes to suffering, no amount of religious hyperbole will soften the blow when someone we love enters into the lonely and dimly lit world of suffering.

Once while I was chopping wood at our retreat in Colorado, a splinter became lodged in my finger. I wondered how such a small thing—a tiny dot in my finger, could cause such pain and such ongoing distraction that I found myself constantly trying unsuccessfully to pull the dagger-like wood fragment out of me. I wanted relief, but I received none until the end of the day when a friend got some tweezers and was able to pull it out. Suffering is like a splinter in the soul that no one can seem to get out. It leaves you distracted, bothered, and constantly reminded of the pain and the unresolved hope that nothing seems to get "it" out. These splinters in our souls are very different for each of us. Some fester deeply and cause major infection that can go systemic through the soul. We can grow bitter, resentful, and angry. We can doubt that anyone cares, that anyone, including God, can do something to help us.

When suffering does the work that only it can do, we learn to lay down our efforts to find the proverbial quick fix and then hang in the suspension of the paradox: God is good, yet God's people suffer. When we "hang in there," sometimes we are doing what we feel we simply must do: endure and persevere, which are among the greatest themes found in the Bible. Read the book of Hebrews. Read 1 and 2 Peter along with James and you'll find letters of deep encouragement written to men and women who simply had to endure what they did not want to endure at all. Through endurance, through suffering we find that we are in the process of being transformed. It is the fire of pain and suffering that melts away the dross and leaves what is pure. Instead of reading great fiction, consider for a year reading a biography a month or perhaps four true stories of how ordinary men and women, who in following the ways of Jesus, lived extraordinary lives.[55]

There's nothing like a true account of someone's life to inspire you and help you move from "I could never do that" to "I want to live and die as she did." With great models who have gone before us, we can learn how not only to live better but to die better as well. While dying of incurable cancer, my friend Chip wrote me an email in which he quoted the words of an old hymn. The words are true when we live the Jesus life:

> It is not death to die,
> To leave this weary road,

And midst the brotherhood on high
To be at home with God.

It is not death to close
The eye long dimmed by tears,
And wake, in glorious repose,
To spend eternal years.

It is not death to bear
The wrench that sets us free
From dungeon chain, to breathe the air
Of boundless liberty.

It is not death to fling
Aside this sinful dust
And rise, on strong exulting wing
To live among the just.

Jesus, Thou Prince of Life,
Thy chosen cannot die:
Like Thee, they conquer in the strife
To reign with Thee on high.[56]

HOW SUFFERING SHAPES THE JESUS LIFE

When my wife and I first married, we bought an antique dining table made of oak. This sturdy table is still the central piece of furniture in our home. This table is where we've gathered for meals, talk times, and together times. Around this table we've celebrated birthdays, gathered with friends, cried together, laughed, and consoled one another. It still shows the marks, scratches, and dents of many gatherings of its previous owners. In addition to the usual four legs at each of the corners, the table has a fifth leg at the center, which gives it added stability and strength.

The five table legs remind me of five core truths that offer a sturdy foundation on which we can live our lives and remind us not to ignore the role that suffering has in our lives today.

1. Suffering will challenge our faith. Suffering can rip out our hearts and shake our deepest convictions about God and life. To suffer is to be ushered into a place we most do not want to go. Yet when the curtain of our vulnerability is pulled back and we are confronted with suffering, we see ourselves with no way to escape what is about to happen.

I well remember when our son Leighton was hospitalized with a ruptured appendix. We were hiking in the trails of the Grand Canyon when he simply said, "I'm not feeling too good." Unknown to us, his appendix had ruptured, spilling poisons and toxins throughout his body. He spent thirty-eight days in intensive care and endured multiple surgeries to save his life. Everything was suspended for those hard days and long nights. The doctors told us to "prepare for the worst."

One night, I fell to my knees sobbing in fear. Then I begged. Then I bartered. Then I would somehow fall asleep for a while. Then I would cry more till finally the night was over and the new day brought more challenges. Thankfully he lived, but somehow everything for both our son and us changed. Suffering does that—it changes the one who suffers and the people who love that person. We do not remain the same or come out on the other end of suffering and remain the same. It is a tool that God uses to shape us.

Another season of suffering for me occurred when my wife was diagnosed with breast cancer. We both felt numb to the news, not really knowing what to expect in the fight for her life. I well remember telling Gwen after two of her surgeries and during her post-surgery treatment that I was scared and frightened. What was going to happen? To think of life without my wife was simply too much.

Suffering introduces us to what we think is unbearable, unjust, and unwanted, and no matter how we pray, barter, beg, or how far we try to run from it, every follower of Jesus will at some time in life have to face it.

When suffering turns our lives inside out, what matters most to us is to figure out how we will survive. What will our lives and faith look like on the other side of suffering? No doubt you have your own story to share. Suffering links us heart to heart and soul to soul like nothing else.

We have to reconcile these two facts that challenge our faith: God loves us, and we will suffer in life. The fact that God is love and acts in love is a true statement we know from the Bible. But it is also true that suffering exists in the world. One truth does not have to negate the other truth. The tension that results from living in this paradox is key when we give up our easy answers and find ourselves suspended in space between these two truths.

2. Suffering produces something Jesus-like in us. Those who have suffered bear witness to this reality: Suffering produces patience and endurance (Rom. 5:3–5). On a trip to China, I sat with a Chinese pastor who gave me a crash course in some basic Chinese expressions. He started with the meaning of the Chinese word for patience. It's made up of two different characters: one is a knife, and the other equates with the word *heart*. The image you see is a knife piercing the exposed heart. This is precisely what suffering does to us. It leaves us bleeding, sometimes so much that we feel as if we will not survive the blow, whether it is in a diagnosis, a spouse who leaves you, a child who is terribly sick, or a friend who dies.

Endurance in the Greek language means "to remain under." When we suffer, we may have to remain under the situation causing us dire pain to the point of no escape. We have exhausted all other options to alleviate the cause of the suffering and have no other choice but to endure—to remain in the grip of suffering. If Jesus was called a "man of sorrows and thoroughly acquainted with grief," then who are we to think we can escape such a title? To be like Jesus and to live like Jesus means to live with and through suffering.

When Ian shared with me his shocking news of being laid off and with little severance, he said he was afraid of entering this season of "trial and testing." I offered Ian these words: "Ian, anytime we suffer, we have the opportunity to become more like Jesus, not just in good times but in the hard times." Ian told me that he had never thought of it that way before—that suffering can help us identify with Jesus and His sufferings.

3. Suffering presents us with a choice. We can grow in trust or we can sink in despair. And at times, both despair and growth in trust happen together. I saw this happen when my wife's mother was diagnosed with inoperable cervical cancer and the doctor said, "You can continue to fight this and you will most likely lose in the end, or you can choose to accept the days and months you have left to live a good quality of life for that time." She chose to accept the days and quit the medical fight. A resolve came over her to have good conversations with each of her five children and her twenty-six grandchildren. She turned her focus to talk about heaven. It was a choice to trust all that she knew about God, about the Bible, and about what really mattered in life, and this resolve bolstered her from long, dark nights of despair. Those times and conversations are forever etched in the minds and hearts of our entire family, because we witnessed a dying woman choose to embrace death not as a cruel descent but as her entrance into heaven.

Suffering and hard times present us with the challenge of learning to do what Paul said: "Think of yourselves the way Christ Jesus thought of himself" (Phil. 2:5). The Jesus life is about treating our thoughts of the pain and discomfort we're experiencing the same way Jesus treated His. That's our model. That's our journey. Jesus is our guide to know how to enter suffering and also how to endure it.

4. Suffering changes our view of life. We will not be the same on the other side of suffering. John, the beloved apostle, said that "it has not appeared as yet what we will be" (1 John 3:2 NASB). He meant that we are in a process of transformation and change. And we simply do not know what we are going to become. We don't know exactly how suffering will shape our souls. Some seem to walk with a limp after a season of trial, while others rebound quickly and appear to have no visible marring leftover. We may become spiritually alive to the extent that we would say this is the best time in our lives, or we may enter a desert time when we feel as if we are in a wilderness blindly groping to find our way out. So we cannot predict how we will change or even how our view of God will transform.

Cheryl's view changed upon the loss of one of her children in a terrible accident. Prior to the death of her son, Cheryl and her husband were "happy-go-lucky," as they told me. Cheryl welled up with tears as we worked through her grief. "Now I know that life is very fragile. We are a vapor. We are nothing but dust." I nodded in agreement, but then Cheryl said, "I wish that I would have known this before he died and left us. I would have lived differently." When I asked her how she might have lived differently, Cheryl said, "I would have not rushed through his early years—the only years he was given. I would have made us stop and appreciate each and every day. Now I can't do that with him." Cheryl was simply acknowledging that she'd never be the same because of having suffered as she did. In the school of suffering we learn many lessons that inform us about how we will want to live on the other side of suffering. These lessons are truly expensive to learn and embrace, but they have the power to change the rest of our lives to look more like Christ's.

5. *Suffering shows us what is true.* God suffers with us when we suffer. The incarnation of Jesus—God in the flesh—does not mean that the skin of Jesus is so callous that He cannot feel the pain we experience. We can take solace in the realization that God suffers with us in and through our lives. The God who is with us is also with us in our pain. God does not turn His head as we live in agony. It is inconceivable to think that God is indifferent in our suffering. We live in the assurance that God notices our tears.

Imagine God being aloof! That does not endear our hearts toward heaven, does it? But realizing that God is with us in our moments of suffering and that He enters our pain with us, we know He is truly a God of compassion. This is the God we love. God is with us in life and in suffering. God is yoked with us in our agony and in our pain.

If God has no feeling or compassion, then we should tear out many pages of our Bible. The Jewish prophet Hosea lamented the strong, emotional words of a God who feels deeply for those He loves:

> How can I give up on you, Ephraim? How can I turn you loose, Israel? … I can't bear to even think such thoughts. My insides churn in protest. And so I'm not going to act on my anger. I'm not going to destroy Ephraim. And why? Because I am God and not a human. I'm The Holy One and I'm here—in your very midst. (Hos. 11:8–9)

To live life as the beloved of God means that the One who dearly and clearly loves us suffers with us. He is not removed. He is not indifferent. He is here in the hospital room with us when we hear the diagnosis. He is here with us when we hear the news from the human resources manager that we are going to be "let go." Regardless of what a company may do, the hands and heart of God will never let us go.

At our retreat, Potter's Inn at Aspen Ridge, a meandering trail crisscrosses our property, which is filled with mountain vistas, aspen groves, and rock outcroppings. Twelve benches are strategically placed along the trail to give twenty-first-century pilgrims the opportunity to walk slowly, sit, pray, and think through the themes we introduce to them during their retreat. One day we discovered that a huge Douglas fir had extended one of its long, thick branches across the trail, blocking passage. So we cut the branch. The place where we cut looked like a gaping, weeping heart, and the tree bled sap for weeks. The wound reminded me of the bleeding heart of a God who gives compassionate care to those who are hurting. It was a visual reminder of our God who loves and cares deeply for His beloved children.

ENTERING THE SUFFERING OF OTHERS

Several years after Gwen's initial bout with breast cancer and a series of surgeries and radiation treatments, we thought we were in the clear. But a couple of years later, we feared the worst. The doctor said the cancer had returned and spread elsewhere. When Gwen was getting ready to go back to the doctor to hear his recommendation, I felt myself sinking into despair. I feared I would be left as a widower and a father to four motherless children. I clearly remember telling Gwen, "I do not want to know what the doctor tells you. I just *don't want* to know. I want to live as if this is simply *not* happening to us." Gwen looked at me and spoke words that penetrated my heart like a dagger yet were rooted in love. "Steve, I cannot protect you from the truth." Her words stopped me in my attempt to live in denial. Why would we ever want to live in denial when the truth is what saves us?

God does not protect us from the truth. To live and to love is to be vulnerable to suffering. That is the truth. Bottom line. No covering it up or making it easy to hear. The abundant Christian life is a life of endurance and exposure to many weeping hearts along the way. The abundance is not so much in our suffering; it is in the suffering of Jesus. His suffering allows us to have life—the only life we will ever have here on planet Earth. Without His suffering, we would be left in our misery and ways that lead to death, not life.

As the people of God, we continue the incarnational work of Jesus today. God's love is extended through our hands to reach people who are suffering—children who are sexual slaves, women who live in abuse, men who were never told by their fathers that they were loved, aged men and women who sit quietly day after day and year after year waiting for the inevitable, perhaps wishing for the end more than anyone knows.

We should not hesitate to enter the suffering of others. If we avoid it, deny it, or pretend that suffering is not there, then we are not really the incarnation of Jesus. Jesus entered a suffering world and so must the person who wants to live the Jesus life.

The Jesus life has a slow cadence that makes us linger and feel compassion for the suffering. Our mission is simply this: We are to remind suffering people everywhere that Christ is for them, not against them. This is the truth. We must stand in the face of the lie that says, "Let the suffering ones suffer and suffer without me." There is no gospel in such a posture, and there is no good news for anyone who sees the follower of Jesus comfortable, safe, and secure while the world is fragile, dangerous, and violent.

To live the Jesus life is to remember our Lord's suffering and death. To live the Jesus life is to reflect often upon His wounds, His suffering, and the physical extent of His love that was demonstrated on the scornful cross. We need to do this because we will not ignore His sacrifice or live in the lie that tells us any other truth than the gospel truth:

This is how much God loved the world: He gave his Son, his one and only Son. And this is why: so that no one need be destroyed; by believing in him, anyone can have a whole and lasting life. God didn't go to all the trouble of sending his Son merely to point an accusing finger, telling the world how bad it was. He came to help, to put the world right again. Anyone who trusts in him is acquitted. (John 3:16–18)

As we live the Jesus life, what should the posture of our hearts be, now knowing these things? No words can better express the answer than those of a nineteenth-century hymn written by a man who had just heard that the wives of his two closest friends had died unexpectedly. What came out of his heart can come from ours:

What have I to dread, what have I to fear,
Leaning on the everlasting arms;
I have blessed peace with my Lord so near,
Leaning on the everlasting arms.[57]

Part 4

LIVING THE LIFE

A GOOD LIFE

Learning to Wear the Easy Yoke of Jesus

You don't have to wait for the End. I am,
right now, Resurrection and Life.

—Jesus (John 11:25)

Jesus is about life.

Jesus' teachings center on helping people live well.

Jesus is about helping people live life to the full.

Jesus' intent has not changed in two thousand years.

Living in an age when religion was oppressive, living in a time when competing ways to experience God were extensive, living in an era when people were desperate and needs were rampant, Jesus came and offered us an invitation to a good life! He described the good life in John 10:10:

- "I came so they can have real and eternal life, more and better life than they ever dreamed of."
- "I have come that they may have life, and have it to the full" (NIV).
- "My purpose is to give them a rich and satisfying life" (NLT).
- "I came that they may have and enjoy life, and have it in abundance (to the full, till it overflows)" (AMP).

How's life working for you these days? My stance throughout this book is that for many of us life is not working as we want it to and thought it would. The reason for this is clear. We've not been living in the ways that Jesus offered us. Jesus said, "I am the way," and what becomes clear is this: We've left His ways and followed our own.

Shaped more by culture than by God, our ways have led us down the wrong paths that have essentially robbed us of the life we long for. And it's not just culture that has molded us into walking down the wrong paths. We've chosen to walk this way ourselves. We've made choices that have revealed themselves to be life draining instead of life-giving. To gain the life we most want, we will have to return to the ways of Jesus. When we live in the Jesus way, holding the truth of Jesus' teachings in our hearts, we can actually live the Jesus life.

I began this book with these words: "This book will help you recover your life." I base these words and this book not on my opinion but on the very words Jesus Himself spoke. Jesus offered us an invitation that requires close examination, one that presents us with a choice to live in a different way so that we can live a different life.

When I give a talk, preach a sermon, or lead retreats around the country on this message, inevitably someone will come up and say something like Cheryl did at a recent retreat: "Steve, what you are asking me to do is really impossible. My life is so full. My work is so demanding. My weeks are so packed, I simply cannot do this—it's just too much." Perhaps you feel like Cheryl. The ways I am describing here are so different, so radical, so much that you feel overwhelmed. But Jesus' invitation to the good life brings hope and comfort. In His words we find proof that we can do it—we can live the Jesus life:

> Come to me, all you who are weary and burdened, and I will give you rest. Take my yoke upon you and learn from me, for I am gentle and humble in heart, and you will find rest for your souls. For my yoke is easy and my burden is light. (Matt. 11:28–30 NIV)

For these last pages, let's finish unpacking Jesus' invitation to see its relevance for the modern world.

First, being a follower of Jesus today means responding to this invitation. You must choose if you will "Come to [Jesus]." Coming to Jesus begins with making the choice to move. Yes, there's movement involved when you decide to come to Jesus. You don't just pray a prayer to accept Jesus as your Lord and Savior. You move toward Him. And as He moves, you move. As He leads, you follow. As He goes down the way, you go down the same way. You move into His steps, and you simply take one step after the next. By taking basic steps toward Him, you find yourself moving into His way and experiencing His life.

Second, in moving toward and with Jesus, we must consider this thing Jesus calls a "yoke." A yoke was a commonly seen piece of farm equipment used with the oxen and cattle in Jesus' day. He used an everyday metaphor to help people grasp what it would look like to be a follower—to live in His way—to live His life. We would need to be yoked to Him.

A yoke is a horizontal beam of wood that has two places carved out that fit snuggly around the neck of an animal. With the yoke in place, the oxen would walk together, side by side and in tandem. In order to wear the yoke, the animals had to submit their way for the yoke's way. This giving up of their way made it possible for the two oxen to walk and work together. Together, they could do what could not be done alone.

Jesus offers us His yoke—His side-by-side relationship with us—to help us move on and through the fields of our lives. You might think that wearing a yoke would be hard, perhaps even oppressive, but notice the words of Jesus in describing His yoke: "My yoke is easy and my burden is light." The yoke of Jesus is not a yoke to anything or anyone other than the person of Jesus. It is not a yoke of religion. It is not a yoke to a church. It is not a yoke to any other way than the way Jesus Himself would live. Other yokes look cumbersome. Other yokes will rub us the wrong way. Some yokes will be heavy, ill fitting, and exhausting to wear. But not the yoke of Jesus. The Jesus yoke leads us to all that we most long for in life.

Third, Jesus describes for us the benefits of wearing His yoke and walking in tandem with Him: We will find rest for our souls (Matt. 11:28). How can rest be juxtaposed to such an image of a yoke? When an oxen pair wears the yoke, one of the oxen takes the lead and wears the extent of the yoke so that the smaller, less-trained, and perhaps younger ox will have a lighter load.

When we bear the Jesus yoke to experience the Jesus life, we discover that Jesus bears the burden for us. He carries the weight of our sins and our mistakes. He bears the burden of our past lives so we can be free to live our future lives. In short, His invitation is that He will carry what we cannot. This is really good news indeed! It means the worries, fears, and anxieties that plague us in life can be offered to Him. We do not need to be weighed down or burdened by them. The Jesus yoke frees us to live in a way that Jesus describes as "easy" and "light."

Fourth, the Jesus yoke requires a process of learning. Jesus said, "Learn from me" (Matt. 11:29 NIV). Throughout our lives we learn and relearn. We see how He walks, and we learn to walk in His steps. We learn how to actually live in these ways. We practice them, and they become a more natural way for us to live. His ways become our ways. At first, our learning centers on some basic ways in which we get in step and in sync with Jesus. We learn to pray. Learn to read the Scriptures in a way that is life-giving; learn to listen for Jesus' voice speaking to us. We learn about relationships. We learn about the essence of love, forgiveness, and stewardship. Then as our journey with Him continues, we learn how to face the darkness and all it contains: our fears, anxieties, longings, unanswered prayers, betrayals, disappointments, and more. As we are yoked to Jesus, we learn how to face temptations and obstacles that lure us from His way. We learn not to fear death, as it is not the end of life but actually the beginning of heaven and all that awaits us there.

To wear the Jesus yoke means for us to walk in His rhythm, not our own. As you know, we can get out of step in our walk with Jesus. But when we walk in His cadence, we learn to lay down the burden of having to live at a breathless pace. We learn to wait and to move as He moves and not to get ahead of Him. When we wear the yoke of Jesus, we can't get ahead of Him, and we discover that we don't really want to. Wearing the Jesus yoke allows us to move in sync with Jesus through each of the ways we have discussed: dailiness, hiddenness, family, companionship, the way of the table, the way of doing good, the way of ritual, and the way of suffering.

To walk in the ways that I have described in this book requires daily and intentional choices. We choose the way we live. We are not born victims. We reap what we sow. If we sow the seeds through bad choices in life, then we reap the consequences. If we choose the wrong way, then we will live a wrong life—a life we never intended to live. Jesus offers a choice to His potential followers. They choose whether or not to follow Him, do what He said, or live the way He described. Not everyone makes the wise choice to follow Him. Not everyone lives the abundant life. Some of us survive while others thrive. Some live asleep and some strive to be awake.

To follow the Jesus way of living life is to follow the One sent by God. Anchored in Scripture and rooted in history, Jesus came to show us how to live as much as He came to save us from our sins. We may have forgotten that important truth! Ted, an insurance salesman exclaimed to me, "I've attended church for a long, long time. I have a good marriage. I strive to be a good father. I work hard at my job, but I never, ever knew how much Jesus could inform my daily life until now. Everything is different for me now!" Ted's realization about how Jesus informs our lives is key. To reduce Jesus to the crucifix is to ignore everything He said about life.

As we have explored here, to follow Jesus first means to turn away from the ways that are destructive to the life we want deep down inside. As we do so, we, like the disciples of old, make the choice to lean into a new way of living.

As we make decisions to follow Jesus in His way, we find that some of them are countercultural and counterintuitive. But nonetheless, they are the paths to truth, and we must remember: "The Jesus way wedded to the Jesus truth brings about the Jesus Life."[58]

It is radical to embrace and value a hidden and obscure life rather than making a splash to be noticed and recognized. It is a major decision to invest our hearts in relationships that we know from the beginning will fail us. It's huge to give up certain illusions that we find ourselves clinging to about people, church, and life itself to live the life Jesus described and lived out in full view for us. It may seem like a sacrifice to our careers, our professional developments, and to the vocational ladders of achievement to have quiet dinners at home around our tables rather than always networking and always being "on."

The call to live in rhythm and to give up the myth of the balanced life is not going to be a popular and easily understood choice. In choosing to live in Jesus' rhythm, sometimes we will find ourselves deciding to spend time alone rather than going out with our friends. We may miss out on fun and be left out of the party. To live with creative rituals in life immediately sets us apart from a culture in which everyone seeks to be alike and look alike. To adopt a daily mantra of "I will do some good today to someone" might make us feel small and ordinary when our friends seem to have much more compelling reasons to "change the world." To choose to love well means that we will move away from the clanging gongs and crashing cymbals of flashy living and a culture obsessed with itself to simply love our neighbors by taking them a casserole when they are sick or helping out in the nursery at church when asked.

As you have read, the implications of following Jesus and being yoked to Him are far-reaching, even into the depths of our souls and all four chambers of our hearts.

If you've gotten this far in the book, then I feel certain you have been open to rethinking some of your ways, perhaps thinking something like this: *Maybe he's right. Maybe if I practice some of these new ways or old ways then my life may actually look different and feel different.* In the end, what you're going to have to do is the exact same thing those old disciples did: Take the risk and try out the new ways. To take this risk will require some honest thinking on your part. You will no doubt have to acknowledge some of your old ways that have led to some of the dead ends you are experiencing. It takes courage to admit such things, but you will not be alone in doing so. Every person who chooses to follow Jesus in the way He lived has stood on the brink of a decision just like you are doing now.

But not to choose His way is to remain as you are and to live as you have been with only a dim hope that maybe the next book, the next seminar, or the next charismatic leader will have the answer you've been waiting for. To choose to do nothing will have a major impact on you.

Think of it—thirty or forty more years of the way you've been living. Is that what you really want? What if there really is something more—something that I have hinted at here that awaits you—that awaits us? I believe there is.

To practice a way of living that is close to the way Jesus lived and is in harmony with what He taught offers us our best opportunity to thrive, not just survive.

Everyone wants happiness. The abundant life Jesus offers results in happiness and much more. He offers us a way to live that will foster an exuberance about life. Not to follow Jesus is to sacrifice far more than we sacrifice by following His ways. You give up peace. You abandon the opportunity to live content. You die to hope and to a better life than you are currently living. Sarcasm becomes your bedfellow and cynicism your only ally. And the worst part is that it will cost you exactly what you secretly want: life. If you never get what you've always wanted, will you then be happy? I don't think so.

So, this is my plea. Lean into these practices. Test them and see what happens. You really have nothing to lose, because if you remain the same, you will stay in the life you have right now. But if you turn and exchange your way for the way of Jesus, then the Jesus life will follow. It's what He said would happen.

Jesus finished His bold, dramatic, and life-giving Sermon on the Mount with these words:

> Don't look for shortcuts to God. The market is flooded with surefire, easygoing formulas for a successful life that can be practiced in your spare time. Don't fall for that stuff, even though crowds of people do. The way to life—to God!—is vigorous and requires total attention.... These words I speak to you are not incidental additions to your life, homeowner improvements to your standard of living. They are foundational words, words to build a life on. (Matt. 7:13–14, 24–25)

Jesus never beats around the bush. Life is too serious and precious to do that. There are no shortcuts to the ways that Jesus did His life and offered us life in return. Since He is the Way, let's turn to His way. Since He is the life, let's lean into His life. Yes, the Jesus life requires total attention. Anything valuable has to be protected, nurtured, and cared for. To move into the Jesus way will require the attention that I have described—and then some.

CHOOSING THE YOKE MEANS CHOOSING TO LIVE

To follow Jesus is to engage in the one true thing He came to offer us: life. To live and stay alive requires us to always be active—moving in the way and on the way toward Jesus, but always in His rhythm. In following Jesus, we engage all that we are with all that we have, we do all that we can, and we participate in spiritual transformation. As a result, we also aid in the transformation of others! In the final analysis of Jesus' invitation to live the good life, we realize that we are faced with the choice: Will we be yoked or not? Will we live His ways or not? Will we live the Jesus life or live our own way?

The transformation of your life begins with your choice whether or not you will, in fact, live in the Jesus way. To live the Jesus life really comes down to the choice to be yoked to Jesus or not. C. S. Lewis said,

> Every time you make a choice you are turning the
> central part of you, the part of you that chooses,
> into something a little different than it was
> before. And taking your life as a whole, with all
> your innumerable choices, all your life long you

are slowly turning this central thing either into a
heavenly creature or into a hellish creature: either
into a creature that is in harmony with God, and
with other creatures, and with itself, or else into one
that is in a state of war and hatred with God, and
with its fellow-creatures, and with itself. To be the
one kind of creature is heaven: that is, it is joy and
peace and knowledge and power. To be the other
means madness, horror, idiocy, rage, impotence,
and eternal loneliness. Each of us at each moment
is progressing to the one state or the other.[59]

The choice comes down to this: To become a heavenly creature
or a hellish one. To live a good life or not. To live a rich, satisfying
life or not. To embrace Jesus' invitation and actually move toward
Him or not. The answer to this question will determine not only
if you will wear the yoke but also if you will live the life—the Jesus
life—the only life that is really life after all.

Jewish Feasts and Festivals in the Old Testament

Common Name	Hebrew Name	Date	Activities	Theme	Fulfillment
*Passover	Pesach	14th day of Nisan (spring)	Sacrificing Passover lamb	Protection from Angel of Death Deliverance from slavery in Egypt	Jesus dies on Passover as the lamb whose blood protects believers from God's judgment. Jesus delivers us from slavery to sin and death.
Unleavened Bread	Matzot	15th day of Nisan (spring)	Remove leaven Live without leaven for seven days	Getting rid of sin (leaven)	Jesus' body is without sin, a perfect sacrifice. Believers live "unleavened" lives in response.
Firstfruits	Bikkurim	1st Sunday after Passover (spring)	Bring firstfruit offering of barley to temple	Celebrating first fruit of barley harvest	Jesus' resurrection was on firstfruits. He is the firstfruits of those risen from the dead.
*Pentecost	Shavuot	50 days after Passover (late spring)	Celebration in temple Bringing sacrifices of wheat Read Ezek. 1–2	First of wheat harvest Celebration of covenant of law on Mount Sinai	The Spirit is given and first harvest of souls takes place. Holy Spirit writes law on believers' hearts.
Feast of Trumpets	Rosh Hashanah	1st day of Tishri (early fall)	Blowing of shofar Confess sin for ten days	Celebration of New Year Anointing God as King	Dead shall rise at final trumpet. Christ returns to reign as King.
Day of Atonement	Yom Kippur	10th day of Tishri (early fall)	High priest atones for sin	Atonement for sin Scapegoat	Jesus becomes our atoning sacrifice at the final judgment.
*Feast of Tabernacles (Ingathering)	Sukkot	15th day of Tishri (early fall)	Living in booths Dwelling with God in wilderness	Celebration of harvest Water pouring ceremony (last day)	All God's people are gathered into new heaven and new earth to dwell with him forever. Jesus promises living water of the Spirit.

*Passover, Pentecost, and Tabernacles are all pilgrim feasts. All people of Israel were encouraged to journey to Jerusalem to celebrate as a community on these days/weeks.

**The Bible mentions two additional holidays that are still celebrated but are not commanded in the Torah: Hanukkah and Purim. Hanukkah is celebrated in December and commemorates the victory of Judas Maccabeus and purification of the temple in 168 B.C. Purim takes place in late winter and remembers the deliverance of the people of Israel during the time of Queen Esther. The Sabbath is also considered a holy day, as important as the yearly feast days.[60]

DISCUSSION GUIDE

CHAPTER 1: RECOVERING YOUR LIFE

1. What do you want your life to look like? How about your life with your friends?
2. This chapter offers several statements to describe what the Jesus life is *not*. Share with your group which one you most identify with and why.
3. In the story about Aron Ralston, how do you identify with his plight?
4. What would a 25 percent improvement in recovering your life actually look like?

CHAPTER 2: THE RHYTHM OF JESUS

1. Read Ecclesiastes 3:1–12. Discuss the "time" you feel your group is in now. Then talk about the "time" your group wants to experience in the next three months.
2. This chapter lists several suggestions to help you live in rhythm. Which ones seem possible for you to embrace and implement? Share your thoughts.
3. What is the difference between trying to live a balanced life and seeking to live life in a sustainable rhythm?

4. Who in your friendship circles lives a life of rhythm? What do you observe about his or her life that is attractive and desirable?

5. Take a calendar and mark on it events, days, and seasons that your group wants to try to keep for the next year. Discuss ways in which you can encourage one another to live out the rhythm you want.

6. Do a study of one of the Jewish festivals and explore how to apply some of what you've learned into your group's gatherings. For quick referencing, see the table that appears before this discussion guide. You can also do some online research on the festival.

CHAPTER 3: THE WAY JESUS "DID" HIS LIFE

1. Individually, develop a plan to read the gospel of Luke. Read his account of Jesus' life over an extended time. Then read his gospel in a different translation. After you finish, find a version of Luke that prints the spoken words of Jesus in red, and read only the red letters for the next thirty days. Repeated readings will give you more insight and a chance to glean what you might have missed the first time. In a journal or notebook, record insights you gain into Jesus' lifestyle. As Luke's

gospel offers insights into the Jewishness of Jesus, record these verses and your observations about how Jesus "did" His life. Try to make a list of His habits, His practices, and His ways with people, and see what you can incorporate into your life. Discuss your findings with your group. You may need to spread out this activity and come back to it when you're nearly finished reading this book.

2. Reflect on Jesus' use of regular times of solitude and silence in Luke's gospel. What do you imagine Jesus did in such times? Since Jesus or any other Jew didn't carry around a Bible, what do you think Jesus' praying, thinking, meditating, and resting looked like?

3. Individually, insert a time of quiet and solitude into your weekly calendar. For example: Tuesdays at 7:00 p.m. is going to be my time of solitude for thirty minutes. Choose a specific place to experience your solitude. Journal about this experience. Were there outside distractions? Were there inner distractions? How can solitude become a more regular part of your life, and how do you think you will benefit from it?

4. As you've learned in this book, Jesus had an intentional rhythm in His life of *engaging* with people, then *withdrawing* to be alone. How do you see this rhythm being lived out by others around you? How can the rhythm of engage/disengage

become a part of your lifestyle in the next three months? Can you mark times of withdrawal on your calendar after the times of meetings, events, and heavy responsibilities? Discuss your ideas.

5. Choose to implement this sustainable rhythm of engage/disengage into your life and calendar it for the next year. Make sure you journal and share what you're learning and experiencing with your group.

CHAPTER 4: THE WAY OF DAILINESS

1. Read Philippians 2:5–11. What Paul described here did not happen in a second or moment. This was the day-to-day life of Jesus throughout His years on Earth. Discuss Paul's words and compare them to the stories you know about Jesus. Note some specific examples from the gospel accounts of how Jesus lived out these words.

2. You read in chapter 4: "Dailiness is where we most long for our transformation—whether it involves losing your temper with a child, speaking curtly to someone at work, losing patience in the checkout line at the store, arguing with your spouse then muttering words you hope he or she doesn't hear, or neglecting your prayers or Bible reading for long seasons. The ability to fast-forward

music and movies tempts us to think that we can fast-forward through the parts of our lives that seem boring or too difficult to face. But we really can't." Discuss your reaction to that statement. Where do you feel you most need transformation in your everyday life?

3. How would exploring and living in a daily rhythm help you in life? What specific daily rhythm sounds life-giving and doable for you now?

4. Reread the section "Becoming Mindful of Daily Time" and explore these questions:

   a. What has your experience been with daily prayer or attempting to have focused conversations with God throughout the day?

   b. Consider using the daily office through an online version or a guide. Try it for thirty days and monitor your thoughts and feelings as you experiment with prayer. If possible, encourage a friend in a different time zone to experiment with you, and make note of your thoughts and feelings as you go along. If you already practice the daily office, see if you can encourage friends and family to practice doing this together. Monitor your thoughts and feelings as you realize that your friends are doing what you are doing but perhaps at different times of the day.

    c. Read Phyllis Tickle's "A Brief History of Fixed-Hour Prayer" in *The Divine Hours.* Do this with your group, and discuss your thoughts on how this helped inform you, encourage you, or discourage you from practicing the daily office.

5. Use the practical suggestions at the end of the chapter to develop a plan for your own personal rhythm for the next three, six, and twelve months. Share these with your friends and group and see how you can encourage each other to live in a life-sustaining rhythm.

CHAPTER 5: THE WAY OF HIDDENNESS

1. Read Philippians 4:11–13. This passage covers Paul's learning about what he called "the secret of being content" (v. 12 NIV). Keeping in mind that Paul wrote this text from a prison cell during his long season of obscurity and wilderness, discuss these questions:

    a. What is the secret of learning to be content in times like a wilderness season?

    b. How does God help us in times like this?

    c. How can you move toward contentment in your life right now?

2. Why are fame, popularity, and celebrity status so powerful today? How do you see this happening within the Christian faith today?

3. Share with your group or journal about a prolonged season of living in wilderness, obscurity, or isolation. What lessons did you learn about yourself? What did you learn about God? What did you learn about other people?

4. What would it mean for you to choose to live like Jesus and embrace more obscurity in your life? How might this affect your giving and serving?

5. As a group, or individually, decide to give something anonymously to someone or some organization in the next week. Monitor how you feel in planning to give anonymously. Share your thoughts and emotions with your group.

CHAPTER 6: THE WAY OF FAMILY

1. Read Matthew 12:46–50 and answer the following questions:
   a. Whom did Jesus define as "brother and sister and mother?"
   b. What do you think Jesus meant by this?
   c. Who is our family expanded by Jesus' words?
   d. Define your understanding of what it means to be "family."

2. Read the words or listen to the song "Orphan Girl" by Gillian Welch. Let group members share their reactions and feelings this song elicits.

3. What attention do you need to give to your family to seek reconciliation and healing? What would this look like?

4. What role does forgiveness have in allowing you to let go of past hurts and to be able to press forward into the future?

5. The outline discussed in this chapter can help people share their family stories. Encourage your group members to tell their family stories. If the group or class is too large, then break into groups of three.

6. How does accepting those whom you cannot change in your family or close friendships help you embrace them and love them?

CHAPTER 7: THE WAY OF COMPANIONSHIP

1. Read John 15:9–17.
   a. How is the love of Jesus like the love of God?
   b. How did Jesus define friendship?
   c. Jesus said, "Everything that I learned from my Father I have made known to you" (v. 15 NIV). What do you think this knowledge includes?

2. Jesus wants each of us; He chooses each of us. What do those truths mean to you?

3. What would it look like for you to begin with the end in mind in your friendships? How do you think this might help the quality of your relationships with friends and with God?

4. What illusions are you currently faced with in your friendships?

5. Describe the friendship you have with Jesus right now. Does it feel like a stretch to actually call Jesus your friend? Why or why not?

CHAPTER 8: THE WAY OF THE TABLE

1. Read John 21:1–14.

   a. Why do you think Jesus prepared breakfast for some of the disciples?

   b. What do you imagine was going through Peter's and the other disciples' minds as they ate together?

   c. John's gospel says that during the meal the disciples "knew it was the Master" (v. 12). How did they come to understand this?

2. What's your favorite food and why? Why do you think some foods are called "comfort foods"? What comfort foods do you enjoy?

3. Describe your mealtimes in your childhood family. What happened in the preparation, actual mealtime, and the cleanup? Talk about how your family would interact around the table. How did the communication flow? Who talked to whom? What do you remember feeling during your family mealtimes?

4. Chapter 8 reveals some facts and statistics about the value of mealtime. Review those paragraphs with the group and share your responses with one another.

5. Jesus chose to be remembered through bread and wine and said, "Do this in remembrance of me." Why do you think Jesus wanted to be remembered in such a way?

CHAPTER 9: THE WAY OF DOING GOOD

1. The book of Mark is the shortest of all the gospels. Before you meet with your group, read Mark and list the verses and episodes where you see Jesus doing good, serving others, and loving well.

   a. When you've finished your lists, compare them with your other group members and discuss what insights you gained.

   b. What was the general reaction of people who witnessed Jesus doing good, serving others, and loving well? Were His actions appreciated, understood, and valued?

2. Try to make a "thirty-day plan to do good, serve others, and love well." Journal your thoughts, people's reactions, and feedback, then share these with your group. Choose your time to begin. See if you could have a weekly time of reflection and sharing to discuss what you are experiencing.

3. As you seek to live with what you've learned in this chapter, record in a journal what you're learning. What emotions are surfacing in you? What do you find yourself struggling with while attempting to do good, serve others, and love well?

4. How could you encourage others to join you in this new opportunity?

CHAPTER 10: THE WAY OF RITUAL

1. Read Deuteronomy 6:1–9.
   a. What was Moses asking the children of Israel to do?
   b. Note verses 7–9. How do we reflect his commands in our rituals today?
   c. What's the real purpose and intent of Moses' instructions?

2. What does the word *ritual* stir in you? Is it positive or negative? Why?

3. How do you see life-giving rituals being used around you today?

4. Use the recommendations for developing your own rituals found in chapter 10's section "Building Rituals That Breathe Life." What rituals can you begin to implement in your group?

CHAPTER 11: THE WAY OF SUFFERING

1. Read 1 Peter 2:21 in as many translations as you can find. (Biblegateway.com is an excellent site to compare translations of this important verse.)

a. What insights did you gain from reading this verse in different translations?

b. Normally when we think of being like Jesus, we do not consider being like Him in our suffering. What would it look like for you to be like Jesus in the suffering you're facing or have faced?

2. Note the five "table legs" that help us gain perspective in suffering. Which one do you most identify with? Which insight seems the hardest to accept? Why?

3. If you're in a group, allow your fellow members to share stories about their own personal suffering. Ask each person to answer these questions:

a. How did you suffer?

b. How did your suffering shape you into becoming closer to Jesus or farther from Him?

c. How has your suffering actually helped you; or has it? Explain.

4. Read aloud: "We must go *through many hardships* to enter the kingdom of God" (Acts 14:22 NIV).

a. What stirred inside you as you read that verse?

b. How can the truth of this verse and chapter 11 help you live while suffering?

CHAPTER 12: A GOOD LIFE

1. Read John 10:10, then answer the following questions:

a. How would you define the "abundant life"?

b. Choose one of the translations listed in this chapter for John 10:10, and share how it expresses your understanding of the life Jesus offers.

c. Choose five words—adjectives and descriptor words—to describe the life you are *presently living*.

d. Choose five words—adjectives and descriptor words—to describe the life you *long to live*.

2. Read Matthew 11:28–30. As you read in chapter 12 about the yoke that Jesus offers, share how you feel in reading the description in Matthew.

3. Of the "ways" that this book explores, which one makes you the most excited to try? Which way do you honestly struggle with right now?

4. Throughout this book I suggest trying to implement these ways and seeing a 25 percent improvement in your life. What feels possible to implement this strategy? What way feels impossible right now? Why?

5. Try to make a plan to implement these ways in the next six months. Share your progress, failures, and frustrations as you move into this next season.

6. What rhythm can you adopt to work on these ways? For example:

   a. I'll evaluate my progress every Sabbath or every month with a friend.

   b. I'll try to read this book with some friends and develop a plan with them.

   c. To help encourage me, I'm going to enlist the help of (insert names here).

7. Read the quote by C. S. Lewis near the end of chapter 12. Share how this encourages you to make wise choices about living the Jesus life.

NOTES

1. *Online Etymology Dictionary.* Dictionary.com, s.v. "recover," Douglas Harper, Historian. http://dictionary.reference.com/browse/recover (accessed November 7, 2011).

2. Try reading this verse in several translations. Visit a site such as Biblegateway.com to read it in dozens of ways.

3. Eugene Peterson explores this in his excellent book *The Jesus Way.*

4. Thom Rainer, as quoted in Cathy Lynn Grossman, "Survey: 72% of Millennials 'more spiritual than religious,'" USAToday.com. www.usatoday.com/news/religion/2010-04-27-1Amillfaith27_ST_N.htm, pars. 5–7, 9 (accessed November 7, 2011).

5. Stephen R. Covey, "Work-Life Balance: A Different Cut," Forbes.com, www.forbes.com/2007/03/19/covey-work-life-lead-careers-worklife07-cz_sc_0319covey.html, par. 1 (accessed October 5, 2011).

6. A list of the Jewish festivals appears before this book's discussion guide. Take a look and see how you might implement a rhythm of festivals and feasts in your life, family, friendships, and church.

7. I have shared more of my monastery experience in my book *The Lazarus Life.*

8. Keith Hammonds, "Balance is Bunk!," Fast Company, www.fastcompany.com/magazine/87/balance-1.html, par. 3 (accessed October 6, 2011).

9. For a more in-depth study of Sabbath keeping, consider reading the chapter "Choosing to Cease the Insanity" in my book *Soul Custody.*

10. "Prayer to Welcome the Sabbath," in *Common Prayer* (Grand Rapids, MI: Zondervan, 2010), 554.

11. Eugene Peterson, *The Jesus Way* (Grand Rapids, MI: Eerdmans, 2007), 22.

12. I explain the discipline of disillusionment in *Living the Lazarus Life*, a study guide to my book *The Lazarus Life.*

13. Madeleine L'Engle, *The Weather of the Heart* (Wheaton, IL: Shaw, 2000), 60.

14. Luke 9:28–36 teaches us that our primary mission as followers of Jesus is to learn how to "listen to him." This command continues to be the mandate for followers of Jesus today. Teaching people how to listen to Jesus is true Christian education.

15. Alicia Britt Chole, *Anonymous* (Nashville, TN: Thomas Nelson, 2006), 9–10.

16. "Nazareth dwelling discovery may shed light on boyhood of Jesus," *The Guardian*, www.guardian.co.uk/world/2009/dec/21/nazareth-dwelling-discovery-jesus (accessed November 9, 2011).

17. *Babies*. Directed by Thomas Balmès. Produced by Canal+, Chez Wam, Studio Canal. Distributed in the United States by Focus Features, 2010.

18. Walter Trobisch, *Love Yourself* (Downers Grove, IL: InterVarsity, 1976), 8–9.

19. Erik Qualman, "Statistics Show Social Media Is Bigger Than You Think," Socialnomics, http://socialnomics.net/2009/08/11/statistics-show-social-media-is-bigger-than-you-think/, pars. 1–5 (accessed November 9, 2011).

20. Henri Nouwen, "August 13: Hiddenness, a Place of Intimacy," in *Bread for the Journey* (New York: HarperCollins, 1997).

21. This word, while often associated with a function after death, also means a total evaluation after the fact. It's an exercise that tries to bring light, insight, and understanding to what really happened.

22. I highly recommend Gerald Sittser's *Water from a Deep Well: Christian Spirituality from Early Martyrs to Modern Missionaries*. The book gives amazing insight into the lives of many individuals who experienced long seasons of living in isolation, obscurity, and anonymity and offers us the lessons they learned.

23. Trobisch, *Love Yourself*, 26.

24. The word Mark used to describe the siblings' concern for Jesus means "out of His mind," which has a parallel meaning of being insane.

25. Curt Thompson discussed this in his fascinating book *Anatomy of the Soul*. As a Christian psychiatrist, Thompson showed how our neuron pathways were formed early in life to receive information or to interpret the lack of information we received as children and how this shapes our understanding of love and being loved later on as adults.

26. Curt Thompson, *Anatomy of the Soul* (Carol Stream, IL: Tyndale, 2010).

27. Gordon Dalbey shares Richard Rohr's story in his important chapter "Healing the Wounds from the Past" in *The Transformation of a Man's Heart*, comp. Stephen W. Smith (Downers Grove, IL: InterVarsity, 2006).

28. My book *The Lazarus Life* explores the connection between the story of Lazarus and our lives.

29. Gillian Welch, "Orphan Girl," *Revival* © 1996 Acony Records.

30. The New Testament has fifty-four statements that are called the "one anothers." For a complete list of these and a study guide to consider them, see my workbook *Living the Lazarus Life*.

31. Henri Nouwen, *Life of the Beloved* (New York: Crossroads, 1992), 45.

32. Nouwen, *Life of the Beloved*, 47–48.

33. German pastor and theologian Dietrich Bonhoeffer discussed this important point in his classic *Life Together*.

34. Dietrich Bonhoeffer, *Life Together* (New York: HarperOne, 1954), 27.

35. Eric Schlosser, *Fast Food Nation* (New York: Harper Perennial, 2005), 3.

36. Schlosser, *Fast Food Nation*, 7.

37. Leslie Leyland Fields, *The Spirit of Food* (Eugene, OR: Cascade, 2010), xxiii.

38. The NIV translation of Genesis 1:27–31 uses the words *rule over*. We are to rule over animals, plants, and every living creature, but how does that apply to our ruling over our health and the way we live today?

39. The National Center on Addiction and Substance Abuse at Columbia University, "The Importance of Family Dinners IV," September 2007, i–ii.

40. Council of Economic Advisers to the President, "Teens and Their Parents in the 21st Century: An Examination of Trends in Teen Behavior and the Role of Parental Involvement," May 2000, as cited in William J. Doherty, "Overscheduled Kids, Underconnected Families: The Research Evidence," Putting Family First, www.puttingfamilyfirst.org/research.php, par. 17 (accessed November 11, 2011).

41. Global Strategy Group, Inc., "Talking With Teens: The YMCA Parent and Teen Survey," April 2000, as cited in William J. Doherty, "Overscheduled Kids, Underconnected Families: The Research Evidence," Putting Family First, www.puttingfamilyfirst.org/research.php, par. 18 (accessed November 11, 2011).

42. "Family Meals Could Be The Cure" *USA Today*, October 2010, vol. 139, iss. 2785, p. 3.

43. Stephen W. Smith, *The Lazarus Life* (Colorado Springs, CO: David C Cook, 2008), 22.

44. This exercise is called the Daily Examen, where we explore our times of being consoled by God through the day as well as feeling desolated by some event.

45. Edward Hallowell, *The Childhood Roots of Adult Happiness* (New York: Ballantine, 2002), 82.

46. Nouwen, "February 15: The Meal That Makes Us Family and Friends" in *Bread for the Journey*.

47. Nouwen, "February 16: The Intimacy of the Table" in *Bread for the Journey*.

48. Paula Butturini, *Keeping the Feast* (New York: Riverhead, 2010), 258–59.

49. James Allan Francis, "One Solitary Life" in *The Real Jesus* (Valley Forge, PA: Judson, 1926).

50. Rueben P. Job, *Three Simple Rules* (Nashville, TN: Abingdon, 2007), 25.

51. Philip Yancey, *The Jesus I Never Knew* (Grand Rapids, MI: Zondervan, 1995), 50.

52. Two recommended books that will help you explore the Jewishness of Jesus are *Sitting at the Feet of Rabbi Jesus* by Ann Spangler and Lois Tverberg, and *Jerusalem in the Time of Jesus* by Joachim Jeremias.

53. Encyclopedia Britannica, Inc. Dictionary.com, s.v. "ritual," http://dictionary.reference.com/browse/ritual (accessed November 11, 2011).

54. View this painting at www.artbible.info/art/large/262.html.

55. For a list of my recommended biographies, go to www.myjesuslife.com.

56. Henri Abraham César Malan, "It Is Not Death to Die," translated by George W. Bethune in 1847.

57. Elisha Hoffman, "Leaning on the Everlasting Arms," music by Anthony Showalter, 1887.

58. Peterson, *The Jesus Way*, 4.

59. C. S. Lewis, *Mere Christianity*, HarperCollins ed. (New York: HarperCollins, 2001), 92.

60. Ann Spangler and Lois Tverberg, *Sitting at the Feet of Rabbi Jesus* (Grand Rapids, MI: Zondervan, 2009), 220–21.

 **Discover More Online**

FOR ADDITIONAL RESOURCES, SERMON OUTLINES,
DISCUSSION FORUMS, AND MORE CREATIVE
WAYS TO LIVE THE JESUS LIFE, VISIT:

WWW.MYJESUSLIFE.COM

Potter's Inn is a Christian ministry founded by Stephen W. and Gwen Harding Smith, and is dedicated to the work of spiritual formation. A resource to the local church, organizations, and individuals, Potter's Inn promotes the themes of spiritual transformation to Christians on the journey of spiritual formation by offering

- guided retreats
- soul care
- books, small group guides, works of art, and other resources that
- explore spiritual transformation

Steve and Gwen travel throughout the United States and the world offering spiritual direction, soul care, and ministry to people who long for deeper intimacy with God. Steve is the author of *The Lazarus Life: Spiritual Transformation for Ordinary People; Embracing Soul Care: Making Space for What Matters Most; Soul Custody: Choosing to Care for the One and Only You;* and *Soul Shaping: A Practical Guide to Spiritual Transformation.*

Potter's Inn **at ASPEN RIDGE** is a thirty-five acre ranch and retreat nestled in the Colorado Rockies near Colorado Springs, Colorado. As a small, intimate retreat, Potter's Inn at Aspen Ridge is available for individual and small group retreats. "Soul Care Intensives"—guided retreats with spiritual direction—are available for leaders in the ministry and the marketplace. For more information or for a closer look at our artwork and literature, visit our website, www.pottersinn.com.

Or contact us at:

Potter's Inn

6660 Delmonico Drive

Suite D-180

Colorado Springs, CO 80919

Telephone: 719-264-8837

Email: resources@pottersinn.com

I AM LAZARUS AND SO ARE YOU.

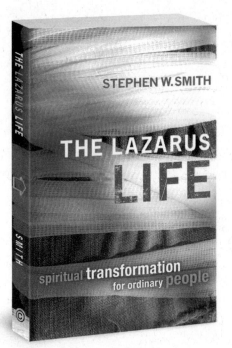

THE LAZARUS LIFE

STEPHEN W. SMITH

spiritual **transformation** for ordinary people

The life of Lazarus chronicles an ordinary man who found himself at the center of an astounding miracle. A divine process that fully revealed Christ's transforming power, through a resurrection that preceded His very own.

But what if the story of Lazarus holds powerful parallels for us today? What if his story of hope and heartbreak, expectancy and disappointment, death and life is our story too? What if the transformation Lazarus experienced is available to you and me?

Stephen W. Smith presents a remarkable journey through the life of Lazarus. Come explore the life and legacy of Lazarus. DIscover a story all your own. And hear the voice of the One who loves you.

FIND **FREE** STUDY RESOURCES FOR THE LAZARUS LIFE AT **WWW.LAZARUSLIFE.COM.**

800.323.7543   DavidCCook.com

David C Cook
transforming lives together